Designer Monographs 3

Michael Graves

Michael Graves

Designer Monographs 3
Edited by Alex Buck and Matthias Vogt

Janet Abrams
Laura Cerwinske
Michael Collins
Rainer Krause
Aldo Rossi

Contents

Preface

On Michael Graves:

Michael Graves is *different*. He's *different* in a way that one might at first sight call "American" in order to explain it. A closer look at his work reveals it to be, above all, complete and all-encompassing in an amazing way.

Michael Graves is clearly a mega-design factory that naturally produces architecture but also industrial designs, packaging, interior design, furniture designs, graphics, jewelry, stage sets and much more besides. To illustrate this, suffice it to point to his kettle.

Michael Graves is, needless to say, not just one of the great number of architects who have also designed kettles. Not one bit. He dreamed up the kettle and thus created the iconography of an old and yet new species of product.

Yet with this comprehensive approach to design he appears rather more "classical" than American. Indeed, there are numerous indications in his work that would seem to bear this out. Yet it would be wrong to object to his work because it exhibits both qualities. Michael Graves is most assuredly American in the best sense, for his work is a veritable melting pot of the different areas of artistic activity, but it also "classical" in the sense of its attesting to a "holistic" approach, to a certain view of the world.

The upshot of this long design career has been a mélange of multi-cultural and interdisciplinary products that will stand the test of time.

The breadth of his work and the unmistakably Gravesian canon of colors and forms to which he adheres make him the complete contemporary designer, true to industry and placed beyond the pale of our so utterly European categories and clearly separate disciplines and criticism.

On the present book

... It's the third in a series of monographs with a special character of their own.

The authors of the essays collected here focus on central aspects or concepts in Michael Graves' design philosophy; although they have all been closely associated with him, their comments are not merely uncritical.

Graves himself has played an active role in the shape of the book. The 16 center pages were free for him to design as he wished and he has illustrated them with sketches so typical of his work, at the same time referring to the interview we conducted with him. The book thus has a sense of intimacy about it; it is as if Graves' physical presence could be felt in its pages.

We asked a large number of his friends, contemporaries, critics, comrades in arms and producers of his designs about his work. We are publishing some of the commentaries here; they provide a differentiated view of his work.

Even if many of the old wisdoms about design have not stood the test of time and have had to be abandoned as they were no longer up-to-date, the quality of "unity of form and content" has nevertheless survived. Which is why this book and all the subsequent volumes in this series is based on a graphic concept which does full justice to its contents.

On a word of thanks

... And it remains for us to thank Linda Kinsey, Sybil McKenna, Anja Münker, Carole Nicholson and all those who have contributed with their statements to the diversity of this book for their collaboration, support and ideas.

Alex Buck and Matthias Vogt

Michael Graves as a Designer

If it had not been for what I learned working with Alessi and Molteni I think I would have great difficulties talking about Michael's objects.

And it is as if a more or less real wall once separated architecture and design. After all, Bauhaus and the whole Modernist movement gave design a privileged position but at the same time confined it to a highly specialized world. It is not as if we did not love these objects, but we tend to regard such things as household objects or at least are restrained in the affection we show them. In short, we strip them of their holy aura.

It appears to me that what is beautiful about objects, as opposed to architecture, is that they precisely do not require complex research and therefore allow us to blend function and feeling, utility and memory, in the way in which we always do with objects we have used or still use.

Of all these new designers, it is Michael who has found a clear, distinctive image for his work. For his objects are not caricature-like or witty, as is so fashionable at present, but instead draw on archetypes, which then inform their respective physiognomy.

I have always been impressed by the way his objects constantly refer to Europe, a Europe that is an American memory: which is why he elects to design clocks, lamps, chairs and picture frames, many objects that together create a happy world. The memory they conjure up is a pleasant one, is positive.

I hope that Michael continues to design this world and deploy his superb abilities as an architect in order to tell us a tale of distant ages or eras to come.

Design sketches for various objects, 1994

Michael Collins

Furniture and Interiors – The Designer of Archetypes in the Era of Post-Modernism

It might be invidious to select the greatest niche in the future Pantheon of Post-Modernism for any one particular architect-designer, but on the strength and caliber of Michael Graves' work, there is every chance that the laurel will go to him, and his office. After a telling and important period, as holder of the Prix de Rome, at the American Academy in Rome between 1960 and 1962, he has been principal of his own studio in Princeton, New Jersey, since 1964. He has taught architecture at Princeton University since 1962, and was, in his early career, mainly known for his elegant, well-executed architectural drawings. His architecture of the late 1960s was, like that of many of his fellow "Whites" of "The New York Five" (Richard Meier, John Hejduk, Charles Gwathmey and Peter Eisenman), indebted to The International Style and specifically to Le Corbusier's architecture of the 1920s and 1930s.

Graves began to desert the "White" flag with his "Snyderman House" (1972), at Fort Wayne, Indiana. This still retained a Le Corbusier-inspired grid, but used applied color of light pink and blue. This use of color was "learned" on the part of Graves, since Le Corbusier was not averse to using paint and color himself, for example inside the "Villa Savoye" (1929-30). This is evidenced by Alfred Barr, in his introduction to the canonical *The International Style* (by Henry-Russell Hitchcock and Philip Johnson, 1931), who noted that "American architects … fail to realize that in spite of his slogan, the house as a *machine à habiter,* Le Corbusier is even more concerned with style than with convenient planning or plumbing."

In terms of "design" Graves' earlier houses, including Snyderman, and Alexander House, Princeton (1971-3), are characterized by interiors which retain International Modern typologies of furniture; that is, they contain metal chairs by Le Corbusier or Marcel Breuer. In his appropriation of these, Graves' sensibility differed little from his American, or indeed European peers, who had all been trained to worship the great minds of the International Modern, Le Corbusier, Ludwig Mies van der Rohe, Walter Gropius and Marcel Breuer.

Although, at the time of his "road to Damascus", his full conversion to Post-Modernism, Graves was inspired by Cubism, particularly the paintings and collage of Juan Gris (1887-1927), he moved toward a return to the order of classicism. This was ripe and complete by the time of "The Portland Building", (Portland, Oregon, 1982) the "Plocek House", (New Jersey, 1978-82), and the "Clos Pegase Winery", in the Napa Valley, (California, 1984). The American Post-Modernist architect Robert Stern has summed-up this development well in his book *Modern Classicism* by writing that "although Michael Graves has remained committed to a uniquely personal, even at times ironic, vision of Classicism – he is not only unwilling to take on the full repertoire of the Orders, but even insists on inventing personal versions of its detail – his buildings have become Classical in their mass and Classical in their essential order."

Graves' conversion to Post-Modern Classicism shadow acts the frisson that one gets with, for example, the earlier volte-face made by Peter Behrens from his formative art nouveau to his ripe classicism. Indeed, Graves' *rappel à l'ordre* is not the only one of our century; Pablo Picasso, Andre Derain, Peter Behrens, Robert Venturi and Philip Johnson, to name but a few, have all at some time or other revised the modern in

Left
Snyderman House. Residence in Fort Wayne, Indiana, 1972

Right
Portland Building. Public services building in Portland, Oregon, 1980

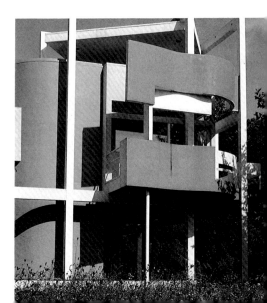

favor of the Classical or Mediterranean tradition. Graves' quest to synthesize the color and theory of Le Corbusier, Juan Gris, cubism, collage, and now, classicism has led him to a rich and catholic eclecticism, rooted in the collective unconscious of Western culture. Graves expressed his approach with conviction in the book *Michael Graves – Buildings and Projects 1966-1981* in his introduction entitled "A Case for Figurative Architecture" where he poignantly suggested that "poetic forms in architecture are sensitive to the figurative, associative, and anthropomorphic attitudes of a culture." He concluded that "it is nevertheless crucial that we re-establish the thematic associations invented by our culture in order to allow fully the culture of architecture to represent the mythic and ritual aspirations of society."

These poetic pleas written by Graves aspired well to the high cultural ground of the 1980s and the era of Post-Modernism. The return to order had been established, often with irony, by architects in America and in the writing and architecture of the British-based lexicographer of Post-Modernism, Charles Jencks. Its case-study for a theoretical paradigm came when Paolo Portoghesi, one of the most academic and learned of the Italian Post-Modernists, organized the 1980 Venice Biennial on Post-Modernism, under the general subtitle "The End of Prohibition", with the resulting "Presence of the Past". Graves was among the twenty architects, most of whom were Post-Modern, invited to design a facade for "La Strada Novissima", a street representing the work of each architect in the Venetian Arsenale. (The ensuing street was a suitable riposte to, say, the totally Modern assembly of International Style buildings at the "Weißenhofsiedlung", Stuttgart, 1927).

Graves' submission was a case study of his theories of anthropomorphic division; the facade had a discernible head (temple), that is an attic story, body (piano nobile) and foot. It developed his emphasis upon archetypal form, that is solids and attendant voids for door and window, and revealed his application of a color theory based on

Egyptian and Classical precedents; sky blue, gold, and terra-cotta red were set, in Graves' preliminary drawings, against sand yellow. Many of these elements were to remain as leitmotifs in his work: an exploration of the archetype; the symbiotic relationship between architecture, design and anthropomorphic form; a reliance on basic solids and "voids"; an approach to symbolic color based on a "Grammar of Ornament"; and an ability to deliver one-line visual puns, such as "temple" for the head of a building. All these elements form part of his "design" work.

If one were to single out the most lasting impression of this facade for "La Strada Novissima" it would be that of its color. Graves is, potentially, the greatest colorist in the nearly-completed history of 20th century architecture, just as Mies van der Rohe was, for example, its most substantial texturalist. The latter's "Barcelona Pavilion", (1929) was a case study in texture: pitted travertine; rich, variegated, glossy onyx; subtlety of translucency or opacity of glass. One might venture to say, in his design at least, that Graves has absorbed the best of Mies van der Rohe while at the same time developing a Post-Modern Classicism, combining an enlarged language of color with excellent, textural nuances. Graves has wisely recognized the semiology of color and its evocative resonances, for example in the "Portland Building", reworking Egyptian and Classical precedents through the filter of an awakening conscience towards the nineteenth century.

Graves, who is, after all, Professor of Architecture at Princeton, has learned all this, as well as anyone who was trained in Modernism is able to. In any case, Graves' Post-Modernism wisely side-steps pendantry in favor of a distillation of the poetic symbolism and its codes abstracted from the longer history of architecture. Graves understands and applies earthbound reds, sky blues, landscape greens, neutral but luxurious golds, not only because he is acutely wise with regard to the past, but also because, he is ultimately an artist-architect. In Graves' case, his process toward relearning and applying color has been highly rewarding – via the salutary intervention of yet another filter to the past, Cubism and "collage". He, for example, used sky blue, terra-cotta red, and green to evoke trees in his "Sunar" Furniture Showroom, New York (1979), although his "Easel Mural" for that showroom is more indebted to Purism than it is to nineteenth century polychromy.

Graves came to pure "design", as opposed to architecture, relatively late, that is after 1977, with his work for "Sunar" and "Memphis". As with his architecture, an examination of the actual design process brings its own delights. He begins with cartoon-like "notes" and "referential sketches" which are as likely to cite in their captions, the architecture of Rome, or some part of the work of someone like Claude-Nicolas Ledoux, as they are to make less-overtly stated reference to those nineteenth century building blocks which our ancestors gave to their children in the anticipation of furthering youthful tectonic awareness. Graves has always been justifiably well-known for his drawings, which he executes with verve and precision, and his sketches for Post-

Michael Graves was the first to show his architectural drawings at my gallery. He was courageous in bucking the tradition of not exhibiting architectural drawings in a commercial setting, and wise to know the power of drawing to communicate his particular vision and challenge to Modern architecture.

Max Protetch

Owner of a gallery for architectural drawings of the same name in New York, New York

MEMPHIS TABLE

Modern design are among the best works on paper produced so far. He nearly always draws furniture or metalwork in plan and elevation, like miniature architecture, and some of these delightful "notes" of 1982, illustrate his Post-Modern chairs for "Sunar", on a plinth next to, and thereby contrasted with, a drawing of a tubular steel chair which broadly delineates the "Marcel Breuer-Mart Stam" classic of the 1920s. This ironic presentation of the Post-Modern versus the International Modern accords with and anticipates the similar gestures of Robert Venturi and his manufacturer, Knoll, who in their publicity photographs paradoxically juxtaposed Venturi's 1984 Post-Modern range of chairs to Mies van der Rohe "MR" or "Brno" chairs of the 1920s. At the same time, Graves' friend, the British-based Post-Modernist architect and writer Charles Jencks was also subjecting the Modern Movement to lashings of irony. In his "Breuer-Jencks" chair he appropriated the Breuer Thonet tubular steel classic and added a pediment inscribed with the words "Thonet Stam Breuer Mies Jencks". Jencks has indeed made an incisive and lasting contribution to the literature and definitions of Post-Modernism, but it is the sight of such an "ad hoc" and discordant mutation which makes one applaud, all the more loudly, Graves' rather more careful balance of a visceral and aesthetic approach, complete with underlying design theory, in his own output of furniture and design.

Graves' fame as a designer was given a tremendous fillip through his "guest" appearance, in 1981, as a collaborator of Ettore Sottsass' riotous Memphis group. For them, Graves designed his highly architectural and anthropomorphic "Plaza" dressing table and stool, of 1981, and "Stanhope Bed" of 1982. Their very titles resound with the glitter of Art Deco and Jazz Age hotels; it is perhaps significant that in 1985 Graves illustrated a limited edition of F. Scott Fitzgerald's *The Great Gatsby*. "Plaza" was made, principally, from natural briar, offset by six drawers colored blue; it had a tilting mirror in its center, with the dressing table worktop flanked by Art Deco inspired mirror-glass tesserae, in extremis, with the whole spangled with low voltage light bulbs, and "headed" by a triangular form on four wooden spheres. The formal values, along with other Memphis work, startled an audience which had been used to Modern, Minimalistic, or "High-Tech" design in the 1960s and 1970s. Graves said of "Plaza" that "it aspires to resee the artifact as replica of both building and man" a comment which applies equally to his "Stanhope Bed" of 1982. The latter began to characterize an increasing Neo-Classical or Biedermeier look to his work of the 1980s. It was made principally from bird's eye maple veneer, with an extravagant headboard surmounted by a circular segment, and flanked by integral glass tables with small "bedside" lamps in brass and glass.

Notwithstanding the fact that both the bed, and the dressing table and stool had very high price tags ("Plaza" retailed at over £6000 in 1985, and had reached £10,000 by 1987), on the level of expensive craft, they sold relatively well. "Plaza" went to eleven customers between 1981 and 1986, while "Stanhope" reached six buyers between

Left
Plaza. Sketch for Memphis dressing table, 1981

Right
Illustrations for the book "The Great Gatsby":
"Cocktails in the garden", "Gatsby's Gardens",
"Myrtle's dog", 1985

1982 and the end of 1986. They represented a return to high standards of craft and production, but at a Gatsby-ish price. They raise the question of how far in terms of design Post-Modernism, is, as the Austrian architect-designer Hans Hollein has postulated, "an affair of the elite". Certainly the appeal of Graves' work, and indeed that of Memphis, was to a radical chic, designer-educated generation which did well in the neo-conservative, monetarist economic climate of the 1980s, before the recession. If the actual artifacts only reached a limited audience, the same cannot be said for their replication as images; for every one "Plaza" there must have been a thousand images, photographs and drawings of it, reproduced in the hyperactive orgy of designer-books and literature during the early 1980s. All of this rather helped the designers, including Michael Graves. In her book *Memphis* Barbara Radice noted "Memphis architects and designers and their friends and supporters saw the fact of being a fad, of moving 'à la mode' and 'comme la mode,' as a sign of great vitality." At the same time, the Japanese Post-Modern architect Arata Isozaki, who had also participated in the Memphis collection sagely concluded "The important thing about Memphis is also the way it appeared to the world … Memphis appeared suddenly, as fashion does, and it had a strong impact all over the world … things always change rapidly anyhow." Above all, "Memphis" served to give Graves a high-style designer-profile; Radice's book *Memphis* gave good coverage to his witty notes and referential sketches of clocks, ashtrays, furniture, the "Plocek" light of 1982 and his work-in-progress ideas for the "Stanhope" bed.

Graves' Post-Modernism looked slightly at odds with most of the other Italian work in the Memphis catalogues, but it did share their emphasis upon wit and Sottsass' more

Design sketches for the Sunar lounge chairs, 1978

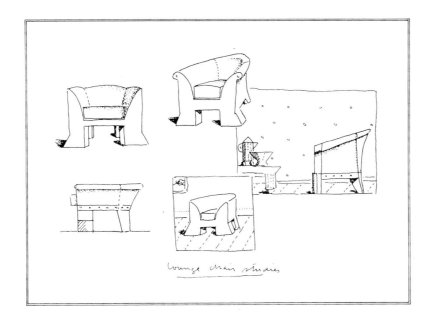

lounge chair studies

comical, but related, anthropomorphism. Sottsass was, later, in 1985 able to draw his own intuitive distinction between Italian gestural Neo-Modernism and American Post-Modernism by stating in the exhibition catalogue *Contemporary Landscape – From the Horizon of Postmodern Design* that "I consider Post-Modernism as a very academic movement in which there can be seen a lot of quoting, especially of their own, American history ... I don't consider our group Memphis to have anything to do with Post-Modern at all, it may be said that we possibly belong to Neo-Modern, rather than Post-Modern. We don't quote from historical architectural elements to give identity to the works as the American Post-Modernists do."

If Memphis had given Graves an international window of opportunity, it was his connection with Sunar in America which furthered his career, beyond architecture, as a designer of both interiors and furniture. Between 1979 and 1987 Graves completed many "Sunar Furniture Showrooms", including those in New York, Houston, Dallas and London. Indeed it was the latter, of 1986 which revealed Graves to be a serious and "archaeological" interpreter of British Neo-Classicism. This "Sunar Furniture Showroom" has been extremely well-described by fellow Post-Modern architect Robert Stern, in his book *Modern Classicism*, in which he commented that Graves' most traditional, orthodox Classical work to date is his "Sunar Furniture Showroom" in London (1986), the ninth such facility he has designed for this furniture and fabrics company. "Acknowledging the English Classical tradition, Graves not surprisingly (given his own penchant for the idiosyncratic) took Soane, rather than Chambers or Adam, as his model. A renovation of a floor of an old leatherworks, the constraints of the existing building prevented Graves from following a conventional axial plan. The principal showroom is modeled after John Soane's Dulwich Picture Gallery (1811), with its arrangement of blind alcoves beneath a series of lantern lights."

This "Sunar Furniture Showroom" in London served to reveal Graves as a sensitive contextualist; a work in London might logically suggest the intervention of the history of British architecture, in this case that of Sir John Soane. At the same time, the buildings of the latter were perceived by other Post-Modernist architects to be the most "stripped" and primordial within the Neo-Classical canon. Graves' choice of Soane as precedent also mirrored the work of some Italian Rationalists, such as Aldo Rossi, who have searched for basic form in simple Neo-Classical architecture, with the result that their work has order without superfluous decoration. A parallel program of research for precedent and context evidently occurred when Graves designed a series of furniture for Sunar, ranging from circular and conference tables through to a group of different types of chairs. The resultant artifacts were an excellent distillation from historical archetypes; Biedermeier, European Neo-Classicism, British Regency, Art Deco, the traditions of Italian marble were all, seemingly, examined for precedents, and reworked according to Post-Modernist principles of quotation, reference, wit and humor. His square form conference table for Sunar had fluted, pilastered legs, with an

Michael Graves had the courage to change and take new stands, even though he had already been sucessful with the former. I'm looking forward to further assessments and the conquest of new territories.

Hans Hollein

Architect and professor at Academies of Art in Düsseldorf, Germany and Vienna, Austria

elegant thin lozenged pattern on its surface. The Sunar chairs, produced from 1981, consisted of: a dining/conference chair in bird's eye maple veneer; a chair with arms of the same material and ebony; a lounge chair, this time with characteristic Gravesian color, blue upholstery piped in red; and a sofa, also with the same upholstery as the lounge chair. These were all "re-issued" later, in 1984, by Sawaya & Moroni, Milan, with a variation to the color and material of their upholstery now in red leather as an option, and numbered "MG1" to "MG4". As a whole these were excellent exercises in archetypal furniture; in his exploration of historical precedents such as Scandinavian Neo-Classical, Biedermeier, and Art Deco furniture, Graves had produced a typologically-correct understanding of the "side chair", dining chair with arms, "tub" chair and elegant, comfortable sofa. They elicit a smile, too; the Edwardian British japes of C. F. A. Voysey or Sir Edwin Lutyens, who caricatured themselves in their furnishings are not forgotten. Graves' willingness to insert humor into otherwise serious design is evidenced throughout the 1980s, most popularly in his mass-produced kettle for Alessi (1985), where the metaphor of the singing kettle is taken to its conclusion via the presence of a whistle, in the spout, in the shape of a bird, colored red.

On a more serious level, Graves' tribute to history is directly evidenced in one of his "notes" for the splendid circular tables, under which he has written "Console

From left to right
Tables and chairs for Sunar, 1982

Lounge chair for Sunar, 1981

Couch table for Sunar, 1986

Book-ends for Architectural Products, 1982

18

table Vienna 1820-30". It is not surprising, therefore, that this circular table for Sunar, with its square blond wood base and ebonized drum pedestal, as a whole reminds us of Regency, or more particularly Biedermeier tables of about 1830.

To place Graves' sensibility towards Neo-Classical and Art Deco furniture into context, it is to be remembered that as of the 1950s it became fashionable to collect and own work from these epochs. By the late 1970s and early 1980s there were galleries and antique dealers on both sides of the Atlantic who stocked fashionable Biedermeier, Regency and Scandinavian Neo-Classical furniture, while the taste for Art Deco was well-established. Moreover, antique dealers, especially in New York, were encouraging a vogue for the simple Neo-Classical work of Josef Hoffmann and the Wiener Werkstätte from the early years of this century.

This was not lost on the architects themselves; the late James Stirling became an admirer of British Regency furniture, and was photographed seated in his favorite Thomas Hope armchair. At the time, Charles Jencks was designing his "Thematic House" in fashionable Holland Park, in London; this contained a few telling examples of antique Regency mahogany and Biedermeier maple chairs, which may in part have prompted Jencks to design his own "symbolic" blond-effect furniture, with their Regency references. This range of furniture was, moreover, also produced by

Sawaya & Moroni, in Milan. Jencks' furniture was highly Post-Modern in that it was executed from Medium Density Fiberboard, a material as ironic for Post-Modern Classicism as Venturi's historicist range, made from plywood, was for Knoll. It is significant that Graves designed two "symbolic" fireplaces for Jencks' "Thematic House" in 1984, as part of the theme of the seasons which was relentlessly pursued throughout the house. The mise-en-scène of these rooms is that of an ironic Post-Modern Classicism, yet the tendency towards relating Post-Modern furniture to its historical antecedents is heightened rather than diminished in the "Thematic House". Nothing, of course, could be more telling for an understanding of Graves' stance during this period than an examination of his own residence. This was a warehouse of the 1920s, converted by Graves in 1986; the result is a version of Tuscan in Princeton. It is a house of striking simplicity; the living room has a fireplace of archetypal shapes, with a chimneybreast in Gravesian red. Real Regency and Biedermeier furniture is contained within, the lighter wood contrasted with black ornaments, especially miniature circular temples, on the surface of the circular library table. In fact, this "blond" and "black" theme continues as part of the scheme of the whole residence. The bedroom has windows which perfectly elicit the tradition of the Georgian sash with the rectilinearity of Japanese tea room screens. The general impression is somewhat equivalent to being inside Sir John Soane's House of 1811 in London, with the clutter removed. Beyond Soane, the over-arching effect is sensuous bordering on the sensual,

Despite an international reputation as an architect and heretic, few, I feel, know Michael as I do: i.e., as a landlord. In this capacity, I can assure even his harshest critic, he is what I have always believed him to be in his more public profession – the most ardent of Classicists.

Fran Lebowitz

Writer and humorist in Princeton, New Jersey

as if Graves totally comprehends the erotic as well as the hermeneutic qualities of interior design, to paraphrase a line from Susan Sontag. His typical colors of blue, or red for the bed-spreads are used with vigor, but it is as if Graves has absorbed, rather than eschewed the lesson of Mies van der Rohe; here color and texture blend well, and with consummate restraint.

The theme of correct Classicism was also present in Graves' boutique for Diane von Furstenberg (1984), in the Sherry Netherland Hotel on Fifth Avenue in New York. A sense of elegance was immediately suggested by Graves' entrance with its emphasis on the color and textural effects of a rosso antico door portal, and dark bronze window surround, crowned by archaeologically correct palmettes. The door portal was itself topped by a telling golden circular segment, a sign that the boutique was by Graves, and also that the boutique had some expensive items in it. The Modern Movement had virtually abolished the elitist color gold from all its wares; here it forms part of the semiology of the Yuppie 1980s, the high period of capitalism when architecture and expensive designer-fashion became part of the same trend. It would be appropriate to comment here that in 1983 Graves' excellent silver tea and coffee set "Programma 6" for Alessi achieved fame by virtue of being admired by Nancy Reagan at the Whitney Museum's aptly-named "High Styles Exhibition" at the end of 1983. If the boutique as a whole is a perfect example of how Post-Modernism and the Reagan years were made for each other, its grace transcends, as does so much expensive art and architecture, the hedonism of the 1980s, through sheer restraint. Graves designed a blond

From left to right
The Warehouse. Dining room in Michael Graves' residence in Princeton, New Jersey, 1986

The Warehouse. Living room in Michael Graves' residence, 1986

Stool for the Boutique Diane von Furstenberg in New York, New York, 1984

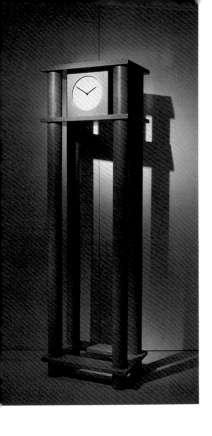

wood stool for the boutique, with saber legs at each corner fluted with characteristic incised black, and topped by a squat cushion with corner tassels. As with so much of his work, the stool explores the archetype, this time of the stool. The "saber" legs remind one of 1830s and 1930s furniture, the popular sources for so much Post-Modern work, but without the military connotations of the Regency and Empire periods. It was issued as a design in its own right, and taken away from the boutique, became a charming and appropriate museum stool for use in, for example, the "Emory University Museum of Art and Archaeology", Atlanta, Georgia, begun in 1982. It works very well against Graves' interior for this museum, replete again with blond and black effects and is one of the most charming and "correct" museum renovations to date.

Graves continued his trend towards historicism in a brilliant set piece, his Mantel Clock design for the Italian entrepreneurs, Alessi, who had been quick to innovate Post-Modern design by Robert Venturi and others in a series of tea and coffee sets of 1983. This pendulum clock was conceived in 1986 and launched in 1988. It was made of ebonized wood and maple veneer, and the whole was, relatively unusually for Graves, "micro-architectural".

This has been a trend in Post-Modern work, with architect designers emphasizing their profession by producing miniature, scaled-down versions of architecture. The

From left to right
Grandfather clock for Acerbis, 1992

Mantle Clock for Alessi, 1986

Dining room in the Sanders residence in Princeton, New Jersey, 1987

Dining chair in the Sanders residence in Princeton, New Jersey, 1987

elevation of Graves' Mantel Clock makes it look very large indeed, like something we might expect in a city square rather than on the mantel-piece. As with his elegant and expensive watch of 1987 for Cleto Munari, the numerals are red and the dial blue. The white face is square, set into a cube of maple veneer, with incised lines which resemble rustication. This itself is supported by four ebonized Tuscan columns on a maple veneer plinth. Graves wrote in 1988 in a small catalogue by Alessi *Four Designer Clocks 1966-1988,* that "In designing the table clock, I was interested in exploring the well-established tradition of seeing artifacts as miniature architecture ... The pendulum exists in the void provided by the colonade, while the clock face exists in the space ... traditionally reserved for the 'piano nobile'. The two figures are then capped appropriately with the head or cornice of the composition. In this way we are able to attain readings of the clock as cabinet, the clock as architecture and finally the clock as clock."

Much of the same, established language of historical reference was spoken by Graves with this clock. Again, it returns to the archetype, via simple forms culled from children's building blocks. It is significant, too, that Graves' emphasis on relative simplicity accords well with the needs of manufacturers, such as Alessi, to produce designs

which are not too complicated. In this case, the least intricate order, the Tuscan, which is employed so often in Graves' architecture, appears for reasons of economy as much as anything else. By this stage, Graves' work, though it had now embraced every typology from the stool, chair, armchair, sofa, dressing table and bed, was in danger of becoming merely formulaic and repetitive and it seemed that there must be a limit to the possibilities of quotation from Neo-Classicism alone.

The "archaeological" phase of Graves' career came to a head in 1987 with his renovation of the dining room for the Sanders family in Princeton. The result was a summation of his 1980s Post-Modern Classicism and is Graves' most historicist interior, according with similar Neo-Classical designs which he was producing for Swid Powell. Graves' ceramics, the suitably-named "Delos" and "Corinth" dinnerware, were launched in 1986. "Delos" is used in the Sanders dining room; it is one of Graves' richest productions, with a star-spangled white bowl, blue inner rim, rich red outer surface with conventionalized plants in black, while the whole has a gold-painted circumference. Color has not been used in this way since the era of Bindesbøll and

Hittorf, and the stars remind one of Schinkel, for example in the latter's gouache *Appearance of the Queen of Night*, a stage design for the Magic Flute of 1815, in the Staatliche Museen, Berlin. Color, censored for too long during the Modern Movement, has returned in the hands of Graves to avenge its long sleep, and now, the same may be said for ornament.

Just at the point when one might accuse Graves of stretching the archetypal blond wood and ebony combination into a cliché, he sidestepped his "Grammar of Ornament" approach, and re-evaluated Cubism. His earlier admiration for Le Corbusier's work, Purism, Cubism and "collage" gave him the dexterity to re-embrace its theoretical possibilities. In 1986, Graves designed a table, entitled "Variation on a Theme of Juan Gris" which is an almost exact, if now three-dimensional interpretation of that Cubist painter's *Fruit Bowl and Carafe* of 1914 in the Kröller Müller, Otterlo, in The Netherlands. This table was the result of a commission by the famous glass firm Steuben to design an installation for an exhibition in 1987, entitled "Separate Tables". Graves has transformed the Gris collage into a three-dimensional artifact, complete with real carafe and an actual glass bowl filled with crystal fruit from Steuben's glass collection. The result is quirky, but in its exploration of the concepts of Cubism, such as the relationship between the second and third dimensions, and the interplay between illusion and actuality, Graves has produced a work of fertile theoretical enquiry. After all, Gris and the Cubists were acutely aware of color, especially the illusion of red jumping forward, and blue retreating into distance.

The table, as presented by Graves does indeed have simple light wood legs, obviously not present in Gris' original. Finally, the work is highly tectonic, exposing levels of depth and plasticity which are apposite as a "five-finger exercise" for an artist-architect such as Graves.

Left
Carpeting designs for the "Dialog" collection by Vorwerk, Germany, 1987

Right
Colour studies for carpeting for the "Dialog" collection by Vorwerk, 1987

Cubism, and its interpretation in Art Deco textiles had already struck a chord with Graves in his early designs for rugs for V'Soske, in 1979-80. These were among his first designs to be produced. His designs for Vorwerk carpets at a much later date were characterized by the typical Gravesian colors, namely red, blue, and golden yellow. With floral tributes, they were more Post-Modern than Classical.

Vorwerk, of Hameln, Germany (a town hitherto more famous for its Pied Piper legend) have launched an exceptional series of carpets, their "Dialog", "Classic", and "Arterior" collections. Roughly 50 contemporary artists, architects, and designers have been involved and the series includes designs by turn-of-the-century artists and female Bauhaus designers, not to mention designs by artists such as Hockney, Lichtenstein and Richter, designers including Thun, and architects such as Ungers and Graves. Vorwerk have thus extended the vision demonstrated hitherto by German manufacturers, led by Rosenthal, for innovating such wide-ranging "collections" by leading

Original designs for the "Dialog" carpet collection by Vorwerk, 1987

practitioners of the visual arts. For his carpet-designs Michael Graves' drew inspiration from drawings by Karl Friedrich Schinkel, depicting finely drawn and shadowed berries and leaves. In the event, the two best carpets produced included one which was decorated with spangled, Biedermeier-yellow and cream leaves between alternating thin and thick stripes, the whole on a characteristically Gravesian blue field. The second had Biedermeier-yellow column stripes headed themselves by a red and blue conventionalized plant on a grey-blue ground. As with all the "Dialog" range, Vorwerk's publicity photographs were superb; the rich blue carpet was photographed

Carpeting for the "Dialog" collection by Vorwerk, 1987

from above en suite with the highly complimentary "Ingrid" lamp by Graves. Interestingly, the grey carpet was shown with the Biedermeier-blond "Marilyn Sofa" of 1981, by Hans Hollein, proving a potential integrity of look between these two Post-Modern architects, Graves from America and Hollein from Austria. Vorwerk's carpets establish a genuine *dialogue* between the ground space, and in this case, Post-Modern furniture, in a rare symbiosis between the floor and the environment of the setting. Graves' third and fourth designs for Vorwerk were variations upon a similar theme, one with a blue Art Deco inspired vase on a salmon-pink ground, and the other with springs of dark pink leaves, with black stripes on a pink field. As so often, Graves, with these excellent designs, deploys a sure knowledge of historical ornament from the epoch of Owen Jones to Art Deco, in a thoroughly Post-Modern classical idiom.

Carpeting for the "Dialog" collection by Vorwerk, 1987

What I find most remarkable about Michael Graves is the "masterful manner" in which in one and the same project he draws parallels between and blends architecture, design, decoration and colour, creating a unity of the visual arts. I use the term "masterful manner", but what I really mean is a rare ability coupled with virtuosity. After all, I myself pursue similar goals with great effort and am all too well-acquainted with the difficulties, dangers, traps and illusions along the way.

Michael's creations are always extraordinary. When I close my eyes and think of his work I see the organic invention of a world of imaginary architecture spread out before me – a Classical and Neo-Classical, a Pre- and a Post-Classical "Graves" city, a poetic vision of life in which the violence of the Modern world has been placated. I see a form of architecture based on the curve that spans Egyptian temples and fantasy worlds.

Alessandro Mendini

Architect, designer and journalist in Milan, Italy

Of the series in general, Vorwerk have suggested that "the home becomes more valuable, and the number of pieces of furniture in the living room is reduced in favour of higher quality; thus this development makes it possible to see the floor".

With these carpets, Vorwerk have been in the forefront of the renaissance of German manufactures, such as FSB and WMF, in launching a range which embraces contemporary theory and practice, while at the same time rediscovering a lost typology of furnishings, in this case the ornamental carpet, which has been largely eschewed or marginalized from the design debate during the Modern Movement. They have moreover, re-established the concept and making of the beautifully designed and highly-crafted carpets and fitted carpets in their "Dialog", "Classic" and "Arterior" ranges.

It is as if Graves is prepared to tackle the larger history of color according to his needs and the context of the particular design. Architects, like sculptors in the past, have often eschewed color in favor of the purity and language of form. Graves is clearly an architect of daring and innovation, prepared to experiment with ideas-in-progress such as his "Variation on a Theme of Juan Gris". His architecture and design is, as a result, made more real, vital and plastic, and one feels that he has become an architect-designer of physical depth. As with his "Alessi Silver Tea Service", all his work in the round has a robust chunky presence.

Graves is, at his best, an accomplished designer of various forms of lamps and light fixtures. This is an area which has traditionally been dominated by Modern and Italian avant-garde designers. Graves usually succeeds in producing a convincing, as well as useful artifact. This is largely because, and this is a mainstay running through his theory, he fully understands both archetype and typology. He has designed some lights which are "micro-architectural". One is in red ceramic, the other blue. The red ceramic table lamp ghosts several archetypes, including The Pantheon in Rome, and the architecture of Etienne-Louis Boullée and Claude-Nicholas Ledoux. The drum of this table lamp is reticulated with segmented circular windows, allowing the light to pass through on four sides, as well as uplight through the top of the hollow drum it-

self; light also passes through its "portico". The whole lamp is conspicuously four-sided, echoing the prototype of the Palladian villa, and most famously the aptly-named "La Rotonda" of about 1550. Graves was, at the same time, distilling similar sources for his architecture, for example his "Rotunda" for the Center for the Visual Arts, Ohio State University (1983). These two table lamps also relate, in their "stripped" Classicism, to one of Graves' more unusual designs, for a birdhouse, commissioned in 1987 by the Parrish Art Museum, in Southampton, Long Island. Though dubbed "Christopher's Wren House", replete with Gravesian play-on-words, there are two versions, one for Kay Barnett and George Clark; both are highly "micro-architectural". There may be elements from Wren, but these are reduced to basic, children's building block form. As always with Graves, one feels here that his theory goes well beyond the resultant object itself. The table lamps and somewhat allied birdhouse dig deep into the collective unconscious, as well as historical presence of the past. This "collage" of history is rewarding because it is, finally, injected with typical Gravesian

Left
Guest office in the Disney Office Building with carpeting by Vorwerk in Burbank, California, 1987

Right
Dining room in the Crown American office building with carpeting by Vorwerk in Johnstown, Pennsylvania, 1987

Birdhouse for Kay Barnett, 1988

Mailbox for The Markuse Corporation, 1990

Lamp for Yamagiwa, 1983

Lamp design for private residence, 1990

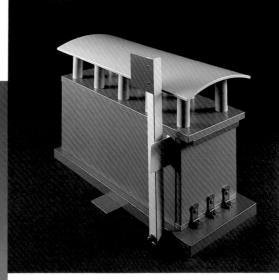

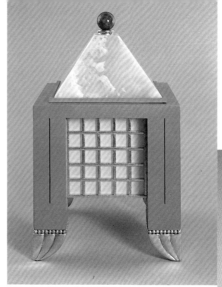

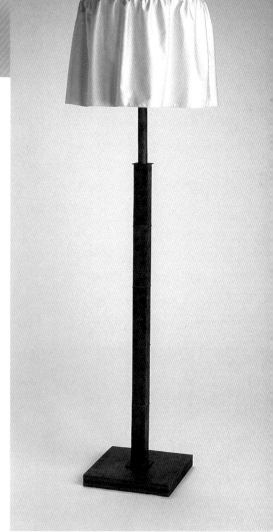

humor and lightness of touch, something one would not necessarily expect from the catalogue of precedents listed above; the birdhouses are finished with a suitable verdigris patina, lightened by a gilded bird at the apex of their pediments, a tongue-in-cheek reference to Graves' "singing bird" in his "Alessi Kettle".

Graves extended his abilities with regard to the light fitting by clearly examining both occidental and oriental precedents for his luxurious table lamp for the Yamagiwa Corporation. This Yamagiwa is an exotic confection, with its blue square form, on curved, gilded feet, surmounted by a green alabaster shade. A light of reading quality emanates from the four sides, through a square form, quasioriental grille, while the top merely glows through the textural alabaster. Part-Western, part-Eastern, the ensuing collision between Post-Modern color and material, and Japanese traditions produces an exciting frisson. The Japanese Post-Modernist architect Arata Isozaki has often employed similar elisions or collisions.

In the exhibition catalogue "From the spoon to the town through the work of 100 designers" Isozaki has summed up his process well by writing of "a traditional Japanese way of writing poetry, called *honka-dori. Honka-dori* is a method of adaptation of an existing poem (*Honka*, original verse; *dori*, adaptation) ... In a broader sense, *honka-dori* can be seen as a method of composing a new sentence or new design using quotations of classical precedent. It is based on the idea that all languages (including visual language) are already contained in a collective text ... It is suggested that the *honka-dori* system should be recognized anew not only as a system of making poems but also as a fundamental principle for designing in a wider sense."

Graves has also resolved other traditions, again via typology, this time of the uplighter, through the intervention of the torch and torchere. Thus, at first for the excellent "Plocek Residence", Warren, New Jersey (1982), Graves designed two useful and beautiful forms of lamp. Both were uplighters, and his notes and referential sketches for a "Plocek Light" of 1982, reproduced in Barbara Radice's *Memphis* book, already revealed the simple form of the shade and upward direction of the light. As eventually constructed, the over six feet tall "Ingrid" lamp (so named after Mrs. Plocek) had an onyx shade, flanked by four ebonized spheres, the body of the artifact being of mahogany inlaid with three brass flutes. This uplighter again refers to Neo-Classical prototypes, this time Art Deco lamps, via the earlier precedent of Regency dark-wood *Buhl* or inlaid furniture. Graves had developed a sensibility towards inlay, and it was thus a pity that the 1987 batch-produced variations upon "Ingrid", made in limited numbers by Sawaya & Moroni, were a much simplified version of those in the "Plocek Residence". The Sawaya & Moroni variation was available either in bird's eye maple veneer, or tinted to mahogany, with a green onyx shade, but without the ebony spheres at the top, or the brass inlay. For the same Plocek residence Graves also designed an excellent "Tripod Lamp"; this has three tall upright supports stemming from a circular, stepped, faux marbre wooden base, and ending with a bowl-shaped glass shaded uplighter.

Graves, again seemingly working with archetypes and typology, has produced a range of excellent, durable lights, specifically for architectural use. This series, dating from 1982 and completed in 1986, consisted of a wall-mounted lantern, available in different sizes, ceiling mounted fixtures, including one of inverted conical form and another of octagonal section, an uplighter wall sconce, and a pendant fixture. All are en suite in brass and opalescent white glass and are made by Baldinger Architectural Lighting. This ensemble intelligently shadow-acts Art Deco prototypes, and though somewhat self-effacing, they are universal solutions to the problem of good lighting. It has often been stated that from "Adam to Aalto the architect has designed everything from the town to the spoon", and Graves continues this tradition. Nothing could, however, be more important than the architect-designer's contribution to the history of lighting. The "greats" of the Nineteenth century, such as W. A. S. Benson, C. F. A. Voysey, Charles Rennie Mackintosh, Antoni Gaudì, and Hector Guimard, all made lasting contributions to the history of lighting, and so does Graves. The Baldinger wall-mounted lantern was used to good effect in his "Humana Building", Louisville, Kentucky (1982), while the pendant fixtures have been pressed into service in the "Erickson Alumni Center", West Virginia University (1984), "The Crown American Building", Pennsylvania (1986), and even over the indoor pool at the "Shiseido Health Club", Tokyo (1986), to name but a few. The whole series is neat and tidy, Post-Modern only in their quotation from Art Deco and use of typical Gravesian "solid" tectonic form. The pendant fixture appears, surprisingly quietly, in the

Please do not be afraid to approach Michael Graves just because he has an international reputation. I wanted some furniture by him and was told by friends that (1) he was inaccessible, (2) I couldn't afford him and (3) he would be too busy to provide a design I wanted. Wrong!!!! His wonderful staff keeps him informed of all inquiries and now my husband and I live happily surrounded by many of his wonderful creations.

Kay Barnett

Client and collector of Michael Graves' objects and furniture in Nashville, Tennesee

Living room of the Plocek residence in Warren, New Jersey, with "Ingrid" floor lamps, 1982

"Palio" Restaurant, which forms a part of Graves' vast, themed and controversial Swan Hotel of 1987, in Walt Disney World, Florida. The commission came via Michael Eisner, head of the vast Disney Corporation, whose parents had once employed Robert Stern to design their New York apartment.

Graves was responsible from 1987-90 for the planning and interior themes of the two luxury hotels, the "Swan" and the "Dolphin", facing each other across a crescent-shaped lake. This lake, and the general presence of water in Disney's swampy Florida, have no doubt dictated the generally aquatic themes. The Swan Hotel is topped by two gigantic, 50 feet high swans, made of fiberglass, and huge shells; while the Dolphin Hotel sports vast Dolphins, and four oversized urns. Graves' facade for the Swan is fertile in architectural jokes, anthropomorphism and zoomorphism. The color is red

and light blue, sets up the usual land and sky analogies, but is patterned with a Vitru-
vian scroll, itself known historically by the animalistic title "running dog"; of course
here it looks like a wave. Some of these aquatic themes are continued or refined in the
interiors, via the whimsy of King Ludwig II of Bavaria, who was "swan-mad" , and
other, fantastical borrowings.

The "Palio" Restaurant in the Swan Hotel takes us, through flags and heraldry to
the theme of medieval and later Siena, via its famous urban horse-race. In fact, this
restaurant contains some relatively basic chairs by Graves; these are appropriately
called "Finestra", and were completed by Atelier International in 1989. Their square-
form back, in the shape of a sash window with glazing bars, is perhaps a tongue-in-
cheek riposte to his friend Jencks' earlier "Window Seat Window" for the latter's
Mackintoshian "Thematic House" of 1984. Graves has designed another chair, also
realized by Atelier International in 1989, called "Oculus". As the name suggests, it is

as equally architectural as "Finestra", this time with a simple, circular "eye" in its back rail. When it appears in the themed "Kimonos" Lounge in the Swan Hotel, with royal purple upholstery it is also in resonance with Mackintosh's now famous furniture, while at the same time appearing as quasi-Japanese as the lanterns and partition screen which Graves has deployed in the lounge.

Graves has designed a great deal of furniture especially for these hotels, including beds with candy-striped duvets, and headboards with stenciled pineapple and palm motifs, with related, themed floor and desk lamps, and chairs to match. For the Dolphin Hotel, the established aquatic themes are explored in the ballroom carpets with their patterns of conventionalized water; this motif is continued on the "Dolphin Fountain

From left to right
Giulia. Lamp in the "Villa Lamp Series" by Baldinger Architectural Lighting, 1992

Verona. Ceiling lamp for Baldinger Architectural Lighting, 1985

Torino. Ceiling lamp for Baldinger Architectural Lighting, 1985

Cafe" tabletop. This motif, of three waves in echelon is derived from that on the facade of the Swan, via the same symbolic form used to suggest liquid, on the body of Graves' splendid "Big Dripper" a ceramic coffee maker, produced by Swid Powell in 1986.

More aquatic, indeed sub-aquatic yet, is the "Coral Cafe" elevation design, drawn with humor by Graves in 1988 to reveal fish, suspended against the walls, one with ears like those of Mickey Mouse himself. These jokes are drawn to their high camp conclusion in the punning "Copa Banana Lounge", replete with table tops depicting juicy sections of citrus fruit, and wall decoration with mouth-watering pineapple and banana. The problem is that the fish, and fruit are all rather too literal. It is difficult to have both traditions near each other, and in seeming to free himself from the conven-

From left to right
Finestra. Chair for Vecta AI, 1989

Oculus. Chair for Vecta AI, 1989

Side-table for Semel Office, 1992

tionalized tradition, Graves is in danger of losing his strongest hand, that is the ability to explore the archetypal. Oranges and bananas are not archetypes, and once the theory goes, the humor itself is insufficient to sustain the design from the serious charge of low kitsch, as opposed to the negligible offense of high camp. It is probably safe to assume given the context, that Graves is unlikely to go further down what might at first appear to be the wrong track, and his later designs prove his ability to return to order.

On the positive side, in this massive development, Graves has contextualized Disney World according to the whole gamut of architectural reference from Egypt, Medieval Siena, "Mad" King Ludwig II of Bavaria, Lutyens, Mackintosh, symbolic design, world travel, and even perhaps Frank Gehry's more than ironic concept of "Why not fish?" for his own quirky architecture and design. Since the days at least of Walt Whitman and Louis Sullivan, American writers and architects have searched for a definition of what constitutes "American" architecture. In all its camp eclecticism and its wall-to-wall humor, Graves has at least given us one powerful description of American taste in his Disney work; it may be the taste-culture of youth, and as sugary as Coca-Cola, and it is certainly lavish and expensive. It is also, like so many Americans, aware of its European origins.

Michael Graves is an elegant gentleman with impeccable taste, and the home he designed for us reflects this. He created a tranquil and exquisit environment, always paying attention to the practical needs of our family. He is a pleasure to work with.

Terry and
Jane Semel

Director of Warner Brothers Inc. and his wife, Burbank, California

In any case, if the "Swan" and "Dolphin" hotels are enjoyable "sun-belt" dives into the waters of high-camp, Graves' other architecture and design has proven to be of sufficient gravitas to allow for the occasional vacation and light relief. Above all, his Disney World work demonstrates the fact that he is an excellent contextualist, a "horses for courses" architect, who knows when to use a racehorse, and when to employ a pantomime donkey. Disney World may relate to a museum, but we do not surely expect it to look like one.

A true museum is, of course, at the other end of the scale, and of these, Graves has proven to be an unsurpassed creator of more or less "polite" environments. Thus, for example, though his "The Newark Museum" renovation, Newark, New Jersey, (1982-9) has overlapped the building of the Disney hotels in date, it presents us with a highly muted and restrained interior. The intervention is "stripped" Soane, with its soaring pitch of height in its mausoleum-like atrium, and in the galleries, skylighting and top-lighting panels which quietly evoke those in Soane's "Dulwich Museum and Art Gallery" (1811-4). Graves' floor detailing is stark and rectilinear, while artificial illumination is achieved through judicious use of his Baldinger pendant ceiling lamps. The overall effect is suitably quiet, dignified and classical, in short a racehorse, rather than the pantomime clown of the virtually contemporary Disney Hotels. Graves has designed other hotels, notably the "Aventine" in La Jolla, California. This was planned in 1985, and resulted in the production, to Graves' design, of the large and comfortable "Aventine Lounge Chair" (1989). It is unlike his "black and blond" Neo-Classical

From left to right
"Coral Cafe". Cafe of The Walt Disney World Dolphin Hotel in Orlando, Florida, 1988

Dining room at the headquarters of The Walt Disney Company in Burbank, California, 1986

Executive Boardroom at the headquarters of The Walt Disney Company in Burbank, California, 1986

Working with Michael Graves for over one-quarter of a century has been one of the most rewarding aspects of my museum career. Michael's sensivity to the needs of the Museum and its collections account for the award-winning results that have been achieved.

Samuel
C. Miller

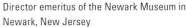

Director emeritus of the Newark Museum in Newark, New Jersey

and Art Deco related furniture, and looks instead like a well-planned, overstuffed aircraft seat, with short, fluted, inverted conical front legs, and a very squat rear saber foot. It is available in a plain and very shocking pink, which relates it to "sun-belt" colors, appropriate for La Jolla, and in a floral pattern, which changes its impact by referring probably to the tradition of British upholstery from Laura Ashley, back via Liberty, to William Morris. Again, it is the prototype reworked, and a variation upon the large Nineteenth century armchair, made available anew.

As with all great recent architects, Graves' work is justifiably appreciated in Japan, a country notoriously greedy for the consumption of new ideas, especially within its chaotic cities. Graves' sensitivity towards indigenous Japanese culture makes the admiration for his work there all the more understandable. We have already seen how,

in his small Yamagiwa table lamp, or in the "Kimonos" Lounge in the Swan Hotel, he has been able to come to terms with oriental culture, and its elisions or references to Post-Modernism. In Japan, Graves has planned or executed many projects from the "Matsuya Department Store" in Tokyo (1982), and the "Shiseido Health Club" to buildings and project in 1988 in Yokahama, Izumisano, Fukuoka and Osaka, as well as Tokyo itself. Not surprisingly he traveled in Japan in 1988, and one of the fertile results was the production of his memorable range of furniture, "The Kyoto Collection", which he designed for the furniture company "Arkitektura". These were launched in 1989, initially to be installed in a show flat in Graves' monumental "Momochi District Apartment Building", in Fukuoka. This block, on the island of Kyushu in the south of Japan, is one of his finest quasi-oriental structures; stripped

From left to right

Newark Museum. Interior of the north wing in Newark, New Jersey, 1982

Chair study. Design sketches for armchairs and chairs, approx. 1978

Lounge chair for Aventine, 1985

of all ornament, it is a remarkable exhibition of archetypal, almost archaic form on a corner-slung site. It speaks a powerful language through the irony of being relatively mute, thus placing it in sharp contrast with the emphatic reference and heraldry of his Disney World hotels. In fact, the building almost certainly embodies a recent trend in Graves' approach to the archaic. Graves had already expressed an interest in "archaic" jewelry when interviewed by Barbara Radice for her book *Jewelry By Architects,* (Rizzoli, 1987), and explained his own designs for Cleto Munari (1986-7) in terms of "Etruscan and Roman" jewelry. Graves had, at the same time, designed Archaic vessels in 1986 – for Steuben, which had in the event been inspired by the typology of the simple amphora and ancient Etruscan vessel, set in a tripod base of metal. Graves has, by extension, searched in his recent Japanese work for the archaisms of their culture and its underlying norms. Part of his quest can be logically explained in terms of a palliative against the hypertrophied excess of the Disney hotels, but his resolution of the archaic may also, more positively, be seen as an extension of his excellent work via the archetypes of history, now towards a new direction which is less overtly and obviously Post-Modern. Japan has been a fillip in taking Graves beyond Post-Modernism. Thus the "Kyoto" range of furniture is relatively bare, almost archaically tectonic in its

Armchair for the Dorsey Collection, 1990
Design sketch for the Dorsey Collection, 1990

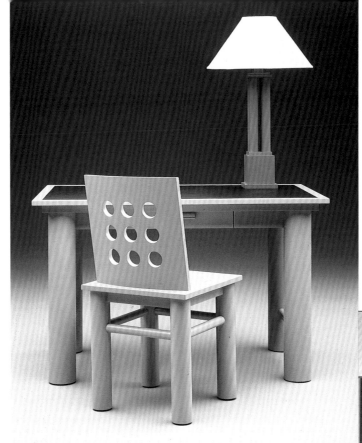

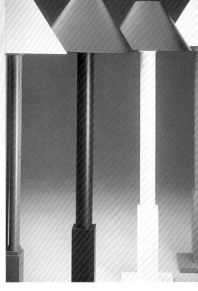

forms and structure. The bureau and armoire consist of simple horizontal planes, set against rising cylindrical forms, an abstraction of Japanese simplicity. Architect-designers, from the days of E. W. Godwin, Charles Rennie Mackintosh and, more overtly, Frank Lloyd Wright, have sought for truth and beauty in the work of Japan. In fact, Japan was characterized by the general absence of furniture, as Roland Barthes observed in his book *Empire of Signs* (1970). Barthes astutely observed the distinctness of oriental outlook in his book, but he was writing about a society which has in recent years welcomingly embraced the West, with its clutter of furniture, furnishings and decoration. Graves has come to terms with this change in his own design, blending his own archaisms with a respect for the Japanese tradition of unemphatic form. Thus, the "Kyoto" collection consisted of tables which relied upon simple cylindrical supports bearing little relationship to the concept of "leg". While Graves' floor lamps for this collection retain the tripartite division of "foot", "body" and "head" so well-established in his Post-Modern anthropomorphism of the early 1980s, these elements are now tectonic, and reduced to a cubic base, cylindrical stem, and conical shade; the same may be said for the shorter table laps. The chairs have cylindrical supports and stretchers, a flat seat and backrail. In this use of robust primary form, Graves seems to

Chair, table and lamp for the "Kyoto" Collection by Arkitektura, 1989

Floor lamp for the "Kyoto" Collection by Arkitektura, 1989

be digging deeper into the tradition of the archaic in order to unearth its archetypes. All this is helped by the flat application of a range of colors to the artifacts which emphasizes the purity of form of the furniture.

In short, Graves has here eschewed the camp contextualism of Disney World, and turned full circle towards tapping the collective unconscious of Japanese tradition, or in his case, a highly-erudite occidental interpretation of it. Graves reaches to its roots, within the Shinto concept "be clean", the simple *haiku*, and Japanese poetic of nature. Even though this furniture relies upon the simplicity of solids and voids for effect and thus also works well with Japanese typology, there is just a hint of inspiration from the work of Post-Modern "Rationalists" in its charge. The "back-to-basics" approach is, in any case, well enshrined in the work of Aldo Rossi.

It is in conclusion significant to note that this more reserved and archaic tendency in Graves' work has coincided with the review of Post-Modernism which took place at the end of the 1980s. In April 1988, *Architectural Digest Supplement* was already asking in an article, "Has Post-Modernism reached its limit?". Decoration and ornament in the early to mid-1980s, recently liberated after its long incarceration in the prison partly created by the International Style, had been out, painting the town red, or in Graves' case, terra-cotta red, sky blue, landscape green and hieratic gold. By 1989 there was every sign that the party was about to wind down. The neo-conservative "Reagan-Thatcher" years have ended, and the economic miracle has more than proved to be a mirage which ended in recession. Graves' Post-Modern work, evidenced by its color, wit, erudite theory and vast range of application has already left its indelible mark. Thanks to Graves and other Post-Modern architects the house can never again be simply a machine for living in, nor the chair a machine for sitting in. As his work changes and develops, we may be certain that, far from witnessing the much-heralded "Death of History", we are, guided admirably by Michael Graves and his practice, experiencing and indeed enjoying its rebirth.

Perhaps the efforts of Michael Graves and I as a team shall become more than a hundred projects. Michael is an extraordinary individual who does not comprise self-righteoness, arrogance, or vanity, compared to other architects I have known. No matter how small the chance and how big the project would be, he has always cooperated with me in profound creative aspirations. Constantly sophisticated, soft, and gentle instead of being a hard soldier. Adopting time and symbolism in his designs with being applicative, repetitous, divergent, delicate, color filled with taste, a human scale, and humanistic.

Yasuhiro
Hamano

Architectural agent,
Yokohama, Japan

Left
Table and chairs for the "Kyoto" Collection by Arkitektura, 1989

Right
Cabinet for the "Kyoto" Collection by Arkitektura, 1989

Laura Cerwinske

Entertainment – Design and the Art of Storytelling

Until American popular culture conquered the globe, only the monarchs of history knew the delights of having their fantasy worlds spring fully realized to life. Imperial Russia's Catherine the Great, for example, had a peasant's hut built for her amusement on the grounds of one of her country retreats. Its exterior was constructed of timber, mud and thatch, its interior furnished with silks, crystal, and silver. More familiar is "Le Hameau", the miniature farm village complete with cow-stocked *laiterie* built on the grounds of Versailles for Marie Antoinette. Here the queen took refuge from the demands and visibility of court life by gamboling in the green, sporting in the hay, and, playing milkmaid in the dairy, dressed for the role, of course. In the nineteenth century there was "Mad" King Ludwig of Bavaria who is more famous for his faux medieval castle "Schloss Neuschwanstein" than for his rule, and King George IV of England whose Indochinese, onion-domed beach pavilion at Brighton, with its

Left
Mickey kettle with sugar bowl and creamer for The Walt Disney Company, produced by Möller Design International, 1993

Above
Disney Company China. Plates for the company tableware of The Walt Disney Company Headquarters in Burbank, California, 1989-90

animal-shaped furniture and dragon-shaped chandeliers, still stand as a monument
to architectural fantasy.

When Walt Disney enlisted his emotionally resonant cast of part human, part animal,
and wholly imaginary characters and placed them in a high gloss, eye-dazzling stage
set, hundreds of millions of visitors to his theme parks shared an experience previously
reserved for royalty. Disney enabled the common populace to step right into a Magic
Kingdom and be surrounded by walking, talking, waving, singing, and handshaking
animated spirits. Like Cinderella at the ball, visitors are treated to an experience meant
to dazzle at every turn.

When Michael Eisner commissioned Michael Graves to design the corporate offices
for The Walt Disney Company in Los Angeles and the Swan and Dolphin Hotels at
Disney World, his sole dictum was "Your job is to make me smile." Graves interpreted
that criterion to mean "give me design that combines sophistication with innovation
and amusement." The sophistication and innovative parts were stock in trade. It was

Above
**The Walt Disney World Swan Hotel in Orlando,
Florida, 1987**

Right top
Foyer of the Swan Hotel, 1988

Right bottom
The Walt Disney World Dolphin Hotel, 1987

51

Michael Graves' tremendous talent and intellect have led to the creation of some of the most striking, powerful, and whimsical buildings created for the Disney organization. The Walt Disney World Dolphin, The Walt Disney World Swan, the Team Disney Building in Burbank, and the Hotel New York at Euro Disney are testimony to his creative skills. These buildings are oustanding additions to the Disney architectural portfolio.

Michael
D. Eisner

Chief Executive Officer at The Walt Disney Company, Burbank, California

the amusement aspect of the assignment – and Graves enthusiasm for it – that proved so distasteful to Modernists, so controversial to purists, and so delightful to millions of visitors and tourists.

Wit, which has long played a role in Graves' work, was, until Disney, more expressed in his art and artifacts than in his buildings. This commission meant having to generate amusing design without falling into Las Vegas kitsch or shopping mall saccharine. With Disney, the fine line between the two was, in fact, hyper fine. Graves met the challenge by "playing straight" with his architectural forms (they exhibit simple Classical volumes and his familiar formal axial plan) while liberally applying aesthetic surprises in his decorative program. Although color, iconography, (and as some have said, iconoclasm) are signature elements of his work, the key at Disney World proved to be focusing on the several and very varied audiences for the hotels. "I had to design for the forty-year-old conventioneer who might take himself quite seriously as well as for the eight-year-old on vacation," says Graves. "I saw part of my job as bringing out the child in the adult without making the adult into a child."

Graves accomplishment was predicated on designing figurative imagery that made no attempt to replicate Disney's literal characters, yet evoked their spirit of enchantment. "The figurative is where the fun starts," he declares, and the sentiment is pervasive. Throughout the Disney projects, mythological creatures, recast in overblown proportions, are both recognizable in their Classical references and surprising in scale. The swans holding up the *porte cochère* of their 758-room hotel (like the seven dwarfs at the entrance to the Disney headquarters) refer to the caryatids of the Erectheum. The 47-foot high swan sculptures that top the hotel's flat, almost billboard-like facade are visible from the nearby theme park and from the highways that feed into the Disney complex. As graceful and promising as wedding-cake ornaments, the fairy tale-like birds herald arrival into a smooth sailing world of technicolor fantasy – and amusement.

Similarly, the eponymous dolphins that flank their hotel are not the famed "Flipper" of the television series, but colossal, whimsical representations of a "classical, friendly, water-borne creature" which, in some locations, harken to Greek half-palmette acrote-

Left
Garden Grove Cafe. Café in the Swan Hotel in Orlando, Florida, 1988

Right
Corridor of the Swan Hotel, 1988

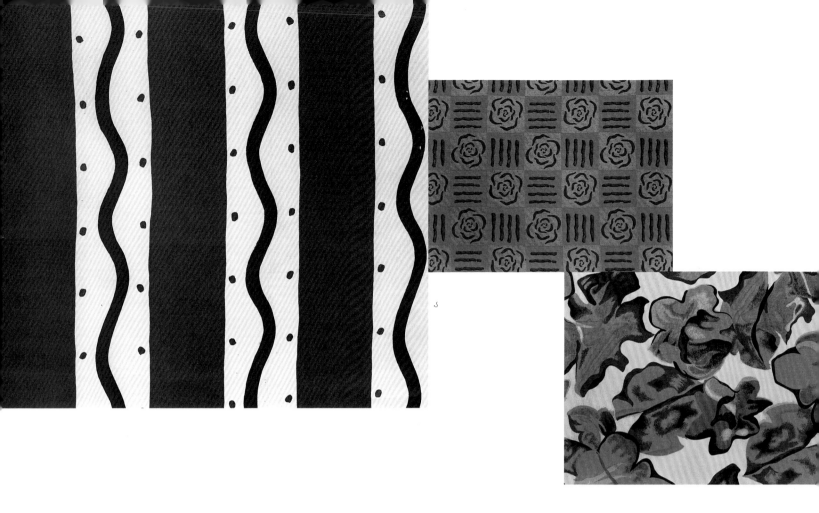

ria. Historically dolphins appeared in the fountains of Roman antiquity (and in George IV's beach pavilion, as well). Graves visually punned on the images in his design of the pedestals for the giant clamshell fountain at the hotel's lakeside entrance by "filleting" the fish – slicing the form to make them look like two-dimensional cut-outs with linear, cartoony faces.

One of Graves's major challenges in integrating the architectural environment with the interior environment was the smooth translation of his imagery from monumental scale to the scale of artifacts. He affected this not only by carefully manipulating proportions, but also by consistently "playing off" between artifice and reality. For example, Graves juxtaposed actual fabric ceilings against gypsum-board walls that are cut out and painted to look like tied-back curtains; he applied illusional, two-dimensional beach scenes to the walls of guest room corridors and painted the doors to resemble cabanas ; he designed a carpet pattern that makes it seem as if lily pads float underfoot; and he repeated the palm motif in murals and in three-dimensional, free-standing corridor decorations to mirror the actual subtropical landscape. As in the Disney park, no materials appear in their natural state (even concrete sidewalks are

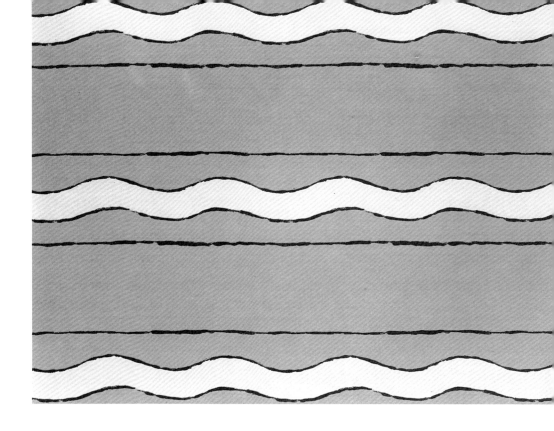

tinted), and nothing – just like the Disney characters – is allowed to age. (Walt himself continues to defy eternal mortality – he had his body frozen so that could be revived when a "cure" for death is found). Underscoring the sense of fantasy, both architecture and artifacts are treated with equal attention to detail.

Graves's variously clever, flamboyant, and elegant effects had to be conceived and realized within the constraints of a typically sparse hotel budget. He integrated that limitation with the fantasy nature of the setting by designing such features as light fixtures cut out in the shapes of parrots and toucans set on perches and carrying electrical cords in their beaks. "Three hundred dollar light fixtures would have been inappropriate and budgetarily impossible in a hotel with 758 guest rooms," he explains. "The parrot on a perch is whimsical and costs $ 25. Sometimes it can be liberating when either a client's tastes or a low budget force you to think minimally."

From left to right
Textile designs for the Swan and Dolphin Walt Disney World Hotels in Orlando, Florida, 1988

HANGING PERCH BIRD FIXTURES
ORANGERIE SWAN HOTEL

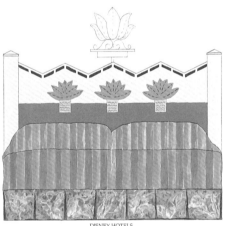

DISNEY HOTELS
HEADBOARD
FABRIC OPTIONS FOR DOUBLE/ DOUBLE
AND KING GUESTROOMS BELOW

As Walt Disney well knew, the art of storytelling lies in its power to lure people from their self and/or cultural hypnosis into another reality. Disney was so masterful at his craft, that his benevolent, sanitized interpretations of archetypal fairy-tale characters as well as his original characters have been universally embraced.

Just as their "reality" is reinforced at the theme parks by some projection or representation of their image at every turn, so Graves lavishly repeated his own leitmotifs: birds, fish, palm trees, beach umbrellas, cabanas, and other whimsical devices. The restaurants and lobbies are prime examples. In the Swan lobby, for example, fountains are shaped like swans, the ceiling is frescoed with flowers, wall sconces are designed like torches with bulbs shaped like flames, bench and chair backs are decorated with cutout palm fronds, and a rippling water motif appears in signage and floors. In the Copabanana Lounge, a tropical fruit theme is omnipresent; countertops are shaped like bananas, watermelons, and pineapples; light fixtures are cut out in the shapes of coconut and palms, and tabletops are formed to look like orange slices. The result of this vast integration of fantasy and the superreal is that for many guests and visitors,

the Swan/Dolphin experience – a theme scheme within a theme park – has proven even more entertaining than the Disney experience, and for one reason: it possesses an extra added element – the unexpected.

The royal precedent of theme architecture was extended into the Modern tradition by resort designers. Understanding that no one wants to go to a hotel and feel like they're back at home or, worse, in an office building, they have drawn on exotic, local, and total fantasies that range from rustic Gothic Adirondack camps to Indian wigwam motel courts to Aztec pyramids to Busby Berkely backdrops. The greatest showman of this tradition is Morris Lapidus who coined his style "the architecture of joy" and

From left to right
Palio Restaurant. Restaurant in the Swan Hotel in Orlando, Florida, 1988

A guest room in the Swan Hotel, 1988

A guest room in the Dolphin Hotel, 1988

is best known for his Miami Beach interiors of the 1950s, the Fountainebleu and the Americana. Lapidus used walls of light, undulating lines, and reinvented Classical forms to provide an accessible, unimtimidating experience of grandeur. He was not bound by notions of purity and determined to create an formal environment that was nonetheless eclectic and fun.

Graves' designs are at once more cartoony and serious than Lapidus's. The mad urbanity of the Swan/Dolphin complex is at once outrageous and civilized, an immersion into a world within a world – conceived in totality, self-sufficient, and wholly coordinated from the outside in. Although his name appears nowhere, Graves' hand is evident everywhere: in the design of the architecture, the interiors, the furniture, the artifacts; from floor to ceiling and wall to wall, the colors, patterns, art, and accessories – from the 28-ton swan finials to the hotel logo to the pink-and-turquoise checkerboard ice buckets – are pure Graves.

A singular vision, a gimlet eye, the will to realize what he has imagined as he has imagined it: those are two of the great gifts of Michael Graves. Among the architects of our time, Graves is one of the handful who have influenced not only what we see but how we see.

Robert A.M. Stern

Architect in New York, New York

From left to right

Kimono Lounge. Lounge of the Swan Hotel, 1988

Star Glass. Prototype for the Dolphin Hotel, 1987

Seahorse Glass. Prototype for the Dolphin Hotel, 1987

Tableware for the Coral Cafe in the Dolphin Hotel, 1988

Above
**China for The Walt Disney Company Head-
quarters, Burbank, California, 1989-90**

Below
Presentation drawings for china, 1989

This embrace of totality, along with his whimsical, colorful and unrepentant expressiveness, have drawn Graves criticism from Modernist circles ever since his earliest departure toward the figurative. "Since Gropius and Mies van der Rohe first formulated their theories about building for a new society, a certain *morality* has been attached to the functionalism of the Modern Movement," he explains. "Truth to the medium became a religious tenet that evolved into a modern disdain for character." Turning his back on that aesthetic dogma, Graves has preferred to pursue the *personality* of a place. And that includes creating total environments, an endeavor, that he points out has become a phenomenon only in the twentieth century. "Michelangelo and Bernini certainly saw no separation between the architecture and the interior. And more recently Josef Hoffmann, Frank Lloyd Wright, even Gropius and Le Corbusier valued the opportunity to design interiors and furniture for their architecture. Their work was broad and not singular. Likewise, I'm not interested in limiting myself."

Left
Mickey Bookends. Prototypes of bookends for The Walt Disney Company, 1992

Right
Salt and pepper shakers. Prototypes for The Walt Disney Company, 1992

By extending his efforts to designing a long list of artifacts and products, Graves has provided himself a greater means of expressive freedom. "My intention is to create objects that will delight my eye as much as a painting or sculpture or other piece of fine art would," he declares. As with his "entertainment architecture," the long list of other designs is marked by Graves's distinctive approach to amusement – through the dignified lightheartedness of a good story.

What most impresses me about Michael is how he has served as an inspiration for those who know and work with him. From relatively humble beginnings in the Midwest, he has shown a generation of students, employees, and associates that with hard work, talent, and a little bit of luck it is possible not only to change the conditions of one's own life and career, but also to shape and change the world around us. Through his own meticulous design and his role as teacher and employer Michael has done both.

William Taylor

Architectural photographer in Princeton, New Jersey

How is your work in product and interior design related to your work in architecture?

Product design and architecture share in a condition that I call *domesticity,* especially when they are brought together in the interior. It is the interior that characteristically portrays inhabitation. It has been only recently that architects have abdicated the responsibility for the aesthetic life of domestic settings, and in their place, decorators and the lay public have focused their efforts on furnishing the interior. It seems that this separation was initiated by the theories of people like Walter Gropius, Marcel Breuer, Le Corbusier, and even Alvar Aalto to some extent, although we know that they were all involved in the design and production of furniture. In the Fifties and Sixties, architects were led away from the possibilities of architecture as an all-encompassing activity because of a trend in the profession to specialize. Today, people generally make a distinction between an "architect" and a "designer". Personally, I've never felt that they are separate. In the Renaissance, architects designed everything from palaces to artifacts with equal success and ease. A good example of someone who did this is Michelangelo; he was a painter, sculptor, architect and even a designer of costumes. He designed the uniforms for the Swiss Guards at St. Peter's.

As an architect, I find myself very interested in the artifacts of daily life and how they can be related to architecture. I'm not suggesting that there must be a seamless aesthetic continuum from architecture to interior, and further, to objects held within. Rather, what I think is important is a consciousness or sense of the domestic. For me, this sense of domesticity informs and enriches design at all scales.

As a young designer, were you influenced by anyone in particular?

When I was a student, my friends and I were interested in people who were influential as "designer-architects". They were individuals who weren't doing much building, but rather, pursuing other aspects of design. I was very interested in the work of Charles Eames, especially in his bent and molded plywood projects. Plywood was the core of his research and it became a laboratory for the development of his personal aesthetic. It was important to us that in addition to his smaller scale works, we would hear about Eames' commissions to design various pavilions for the United States at international exhibitions. He was an admired architect, as well as a designer considered to be in the same league as Walter Dorwin Teague and Raymond Loewy. And yet, he wasn't much older than we were. We felt that we could identify with him and the way he went about his work. Probably because there was nothing cold about it – it had its own life.

You have developed overall concepts for various companies, such as Lenox. Could you tell us how this came about?

Well, Lenox is something we didn't expect would work out as it did. You see, what we were really interested in was an architectural commission; the addition to their home office in New Jersey. They were interviewing graphic artists to give them a new packaging identity. Somehow we managed to get in there. We showed them what we had done for exhibitions, posters, books and book-cover designs. Sometimes I think we got the job because we were more animated than the graphic design firms we were competing against. At the time we also expressed our interest in becoming involved with them on a long-term basis. We soon found out that the home office pro-

ject had already been given to another architect. Well, we thought that we were left empty-handed, but to our surprise, they turned around and asked us if we would consider doing a showroom for them. Out of that came Lenox at Bloomingdale's and the corporate identity "package" – the logo, colors, boxes, bags, and so on. Following that there were several other installations at their boutiques around the world, a construction guide for displays at annual merchandise fairs and a manual of plans for a variety of retail situations. It turned out to be an interesting and profitable project that led us into areas of design we hadn't considered before.

How would you describe your work for Walt Disney? Does it constitute an interface between architecture, design and entertainment?

A Disney project is of course, all of those things. But as an architect, what's most interesting about Disney is how you can make something which is themed seem like it's not.
The challenge is to make everything from a carpet to a light fixture contribute to the character and theme of a place, without being too literal. When an animal – a seahorse or a fish – was employed

to hold the glass bowl of a light fixture in one of the hotels, we tried to abstract it by making it planar instead of three-dimensional, just as Matisse might have drawn a line and then repeated it again and again so that eventually, through its repetition, it became mechanical, an interpretation. Disney has its own in-house iconography – it's firmly established and well understood. Because of this, there are many opportunities to abstract theme and character in its buildings. That's what interested me the most in those projects, more so than the crossover between architecture, design and entertainment.

Given that you are all too aware of just how fragmented training in design usually is, how do you approach teaching - especially in your capacity as a professor at Princeton University?

Well, I've taught for over thirty years, and I know that there was a time when you could find, at least in certain schools of architecture, a greater consensus with respect to educating an architect. I also think that during that time, more was taught and learned. As architectural design has become more pluralized, the teaching of it has reacted similarly; it's become very difficult. The effect is that when people arrive at graduate school today, and Princeton is no exception, they can't all start at the same point. Their architectural educations have been so diverse. Now is a challenging time to be a teacher and to be involved in the architectural debate. You need to have a firm belief in what architecture is to you, and then you have to know how to get your message across. I've lately found myself in situations where students can't even begin to communicate about architecture because they have little or no idea that architecture is a language. I know it's a cycle – and cycles continue. We're in a period of history where there is no consensus at all. I can say "Humanism", and so can Norman Foster. He can reason that he conceives his buildings from a humanistic point of view and so can I. It confirms the power of words in architecture today. To me though, it doesn't seem possible that all things are the same. I acknowledge that we live in a homogenous world, but I still think that without some distinction it becomes meaningless. For example, it would be great if we could begin by agreeing on what a street is, what a town square is, a door or a window.

The first thing that new students at Princeton think about when they begin a project is how they can break its rules. Unfortunately, it's tough to break the rules when you don't have any idea of what those rules are. I think it's part of the attitude that students arrive with – that they are going to be the next architectural genius; the next x, y, or z. And sometimes they give more

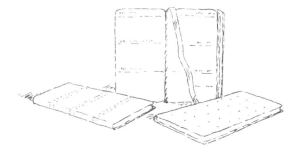

thought to that than to learning and understanding the languages of architecture: artistically, philosophically, technically, and fundamentally. I imagine it's a problem everywhere. Our society teaches us that unless you are an original, you are nothing. Architecture doesn't really have a lot to do with originality on its own. It has to do with originality within language. It operates very much like good literature, yet if you don't know the vocabulary, you won't be able to put a sentence together.

How would you describe the way you treat history?

I think it's important to know that you're not "treating" or "employing" history, but rather you're participating in its continuities, both cultural and strategic. It's important that history isn't seen simply as a "storehouse" of forms. The history comes from the forms themselves and how they're understood symbolically, pragmatically, and stylistically. These, in turn, have affected our thinking and our own inventions. You're not using the grab-bag of history – a real criticism of some post-modernists – but simply seeing that you're a part of a continuous culture – just as music, literature, and painting all are. Every culture has its rifts, its changes, its moments of reevaluation. I think we're in one of those periods right now. If you were to examine classicism from the 4th or 5th century BC to the present day, you would find there to be only two major breaks, one being Gothic and the other, Modernism. Both have influenced classicism and I presume they will continue to do so. When most laymen think about Classicism, they don't think of it as a classification of buildings and their relation to their surroundings. They think of it only in terms of a style. I find it unfortunate that this has happened. But it's no surprise when you realize how many people are still conditioned by the break insisted upon by Walter Gropius and the Modernists. It's prevented them from appreciating the continuities of the architectural tradition. At the same time, it's been so successful that most people are unaware of the reason or purpose for the break in the first place. I believe it is this misunderstanding which leads people to think that history is out there and you can either ignore it or use it.

Unlike in the U.S., you are known in Europe above all as a product designer, not as an architect. There is hardly a table without some object designed by you on it. How do you explain this difference?

I can think of two reasons for why this has happened. The first one has to do with volume. We've done much more tableware for the European market than we have for the American market. We've designed over 100 pieces for Alessi alone. Although Alessi products are available in the United States, the distribution isn't as wide as it is in Europe. Much more is available there. The other reason has to do with the market itself. In Europe you find a sensibility to design, specifically in the middle classes, that has never existed in the U.S. It can be seen in everything from the way people dress to the way they assemble their interiors, to the objects they collect. I suppose that this attitude just never took root in the U.S. the way that it did in Europe. It exists, but to a much lesser degree. Good design is not an important issue to the majority of Americans when they set about creating their environments. An example I can give you for this can be found in the way that people dress. For instance, if a clerk in Rome makes a minimum wage, he or she will spend the necessary money on one good set of clothes – a suit, a dress, whatever – as opposed to shopping frequently and for many things as their counterparts here in the U.S. might do. One buys for variety's sake and gets a greater selection, the other buys one fine blue suit that they can wear every day and looks the best that they can.

What do you feel is the difference between companies who commission your work in the U.S., such as Atelier International, and those in Europe such as Alessi?

There isn't a lot of difference between them. The process is very much the same because the people from those companies have similar intentions whether they hire me, or someone else. To start with, if I am hired, it's because the company is interested in design. There is an understanding that this interest will be translated into a product of high quality. They both require similar services; they both operate as large companies who have many dealings with people like myself. They always conduct themselves professionally. So, in fact, I don't see much difference; instead I see similarity.

You have designed a whole series of items of table and kitchenware for Alessi. How did this come about and what experiences did you have in the course of that collaboration?

Well that's a book unto itself …
The story begins with Alberto Alessi asking a dozen or so architects from around the world to design a sterling silver tea service. I remember there were several Americans – Stern, Meier, and myself and others such as Rossi and Izosaki. The object of the exercise was not to sell tea sets, but much more simply, to bring the Alessi name to the United States, and perhaps other places in Europe and Asia as well. I think that this marketing idea of Alessi's was really quite brilliant.

Following our designs, Alessi made these very expensive tea services and displayed them not in stores but in museums. Any museum that had the pretension or prospect of having a future design collection wanted to show them. The Museum of Modern Art didn't take the exhibit but the Metropolitan Museum of Art did, and that was a kind of coup. Alessi was careful; he made sure that the collection was always shown in a small, gently lit room; an exhibition unto itself. When shown in private galleries like Max Protetch in New York, the tea services were offered for sale. Well, much to everyone's surprise, they started to sell, and ours sold – I believe – better than anyone else's. Obviously, I've lost count now, though I think that they sold forty or so sets at about 25 or 35 thousand dollars each. It got to the point where the Reagan White House asked for one to be donated but Alessi wouldn't agree to it. Anyhow, Alessi came back to us with a new project. He wanted an American to design a teakettle specifically for the American market. He thought that they would sell a lot of kettles in the U.S. and only a marginal number in Europe. Americans, I remember him telling me, boil water for instant coffee. Europeans, on the other hand, use an espresso maker almost exclusively. For Alessi, the kettle wasn't necessary for Italy, Spain, or France, except when those people had their occasional cup of tea. As it turns out though, equal numbers of the kettle have been sold in Europe and America. So there you go. Good news for Alessi and good news for us; especially for a teakettle that hasn't exhausted its sales as yet.

The working relationship with Alessi on the teakettle was very different from that of the tea service. There was absolute "carte blanche" with the tea set. The teakettle was definitely not like

that. It was designed to correct the mistakes of previous kettles whose handles hung over their bodies, causing them to burn if not placed squarely on the flame. Or the kettle that took so long to boil because not enough water was at its base, or even the one that was difficult to lift because the volume wasn't correct for its size. These were the primary issues, the design rules that had to be considered when we began the project. For us, the shape of the kettle, a kind of cone, became the smartest for getting the most out of the volume and its proximity to the flame. Once that was decided, everything else began to fall into place. During this time I was trying to decide on the character of the kettle. I wanted something a little lighthearted, not so serious. That's how I became fascinated with the idea of the bird. Wouldn't it be interesting I thought, if I could use water to animate the little bird perched on the end of the spout? I suppose that's how it all came about.

I'm reminded of a charming letter that I received from a French author a few years ago. Although I've forgotten his name, I remember his note. In it he explained that he worked in his home and every morning to begin his day, he would boil water for his tea in my kettle. Every morning, he said, it made him smile, and that was the reason for his letter. To me that letter confirmed that my hopes for the teakettle had been realized.

Well, as the kettle sold, we started to move into producing a wider range of objects, something that Alessi named the "Graves Family". Today, we continue to work with them but we're moving away from that original family and are instead focusing on other families in the Alessi tradition. It has actually become more interesting, in that there are lots of refinements and design adjustments that we can make on different objects. Of course they're of a similar sort, but the parameters of our original scheme – the shape of the handle and the colors – have been replaced by new ones. I find that our work with Alessi is even more fruitful now that we've expanded our range and I suppose Alessi has expanded the way that they think of us in their range of designers. It has grown from stainless steel to blackware to porcelain to flatware to glass to plastic. For example we're now designing two different patterns for dinnerware. If we can release one or two patterns a year, we'll have a very nice range of things within a short time. It becomes mutually beneficial, for us and for Alessi.

As time goes by, I think that Alessi sees us to be acceptable to a larger and larger cross-section of people, more so for instance, than work that is either of a higher style or a higher price.

A Frank Gehry teakettle, which is around three times the price of ours, will interest a certain number of people, but it won't be for everybody. Our's isn't for everybody either, but it has a wider audience. It's very smart marketing on Alessi's part to have the kind of attention a kettle like Frank's will bring. Alessi has a very clear idea about his family of teakettles, and we take it very seriously.

The "Tea and Coffee Piazza" for Alessi triggered a discussion that challenged conceptions of design and blurred the distinctions between design and architecture. How do you distinguish between architectural design and product design today?

Aside from obvious differences in program, I really don't distinguish between architecture and design. To me, the idea begins with classicism, a language that's perceived in particular landscapes and cities, and is born out of notions of symbolism and pragmatism and, as we know, Humanism. It has a clear relationship to the body and to our psyche of public and private spaces. This "humanistic" approach directs me in making buildings as well as objects. I suppose that is where the overlap occurs. You think about how you're going to put your hand on the grip of a kettle in the same way that you think about the placement of your hand on the pull of a door. How you might move with that kettle in your grasp could be seen as similar to the physical action and the psychological condition of going through a door and moving across its threshold. I like to consider architecture from the point of view of the still life.

Between buildings and objects there are similarities in ideas of arrangement, ideas of proportion, construction and ornamentation. The differences come with scale – the scale of the landscape, the scale of the interior. When you look at the recent history of design, from the early 1900's to the present, something like the location of the handle isn't necessarily an issue in a design's overall makeup. Instead, it was the appearance of the piece or the metaphor that was conjured, or the personal interest of the artist, architect or designer; that's what was at issue. I guess I don't seek to

make such statements through my work. I don't want it to suggest some hyper-condition of the machine or space travel. I want it to be understood and useful for what it is.

Whether it's a library or a tea set, I always begin a project by thinking about use and symbol simultaneously. This comes from a long history of not wanting to be called by a client in the middle of the night who says, "my roof is leaking", which is something that did happen in my early career. Similarly, I don't want Mr. Alessi calling to say, "the handle is burnt". With luck you find the place where use and symbol are not separate issues. You don't want to compromise your intentions or the eventual object itself. I call it "keeping the rain out".

The issue of shift in scale seems to be very important for your work. In your designs, how do changes in dimension affect an object's character?

Before answering this question, I think it's important to clarify the term *scale*. People, especially architects and architectural critics often refer to the *size* or *scale* of the architecture as if they were the same thing. The word scale has to do with relationships, the relationships of the human body to its context and the objects within it. For instance, a discussion of scale would be appropriate if we were determining a suitable size for the handle of a tea kettle as it would be used by the hand as opposed to something that would be used for the entire arm, or the entire body. Size has little to do with relationships. Size can be measured, documented. Both size and scale help us understand our world, yet one is quantitative and abstract while the other is qualitative and tactile. This clarification is important to me because it helps to define how I go about making things. I consider what is appropriate to the hand or the body, the window or the wall. If you think of the still life question again, as it might be applied to architecture, the way a body approaches a series of buildings in the landscape is not unlike the hand or the eye of a person sitting at a table approaching a glass or a pitcher or a plate. Though my examples vary in their significance, the mental state of the individual approaching those places in their daily rituals is the same.

Although you are repeatedly termed a typically American designer, much of your work is based on a classical, southern European canon of forms. Do you believe that this formal language is the right answer to design questions at the end of the 20th century?

I never think about architecture or design in that way. I believe that the real changes of the 20th century have occurred where technology has touched us. Certain changes can occur when technology allows us to do things that were once thought to be impossible. As we create new things we eliminate the old. As I've said before, architecture is a language of forms. Like any other language it grows and adapts, but essentially it remains the same. However, one example that would offer a challenge to this idea is the candle. We don't need to use them, but we do. We enjoy the flame's warmth and its special kind of light. It isn't pragmatically necessary, but socially it's an agreeable thing to do; it's romantic. It's a convention that we have a hard time giving up even though we have other more sophisticated means of warming and illuminating a room. I suppose the reason we haven't given up on the candle is because we'd be missing out on the magic of the experience.

A large number of your designs are immediately recognizable by the colors you use. What is the concept involved here?

The colors that I've used in buildings and the symbols that they represent generally deal with the landscape. If a building needs to be firmly rooted in the landscape, I might use colors that are heavier at the base, colors that are suggestive of the earth – terra cottas for instance. For me, as a building gets closer to the sky, it gets lighter. To make it appear, and ostensibly *be* lighter, I gradually incorporate lighter colors into the palette. This doesn't mean that the higher reaches of a building need to be blue, but it might be appropriate to use colors which one could call more ephemeral. While this makes sense in terms of the representation of a landscape in an abstracted way, it could also be argued that if for one reason or another you wanted to invert the language, put that which is heavy on top, with the light on the bottom, it could still be understood as long as you are not using a neutral language. I think it is always important to remember that a visual language should not exceed the grasp of the casual observer; all is lost if it cannot be understood.
I think that this idea of a symbolic language of color is just as relevant in the design of products as it is in the design of architecture. For instance, if I were to begin making an object, whether it's a candelabra or a ceramic piece like the Big Dripper, I might consider it in two ways. The first would

be to think of the form alone, as a three dimensional tabula rasa, then to apply color to its surface. The other way would be to think of color and form as inseparable from each other. In this way, form and color are joined through symbol, and can be understood as components of a greater language. For me, no matter what the subject or the scale, form and color are integrated in one continuous thought.

I was in Japan for the opening of a building we had done, and somebody asked me if I could explain the colors I had used for its facades. I began by explaining that there is the context of other offices and towers, that it's situated on the bay of the Sea of Japan and that our particular building is the one closest to the water. The relationship between the building and the water might then be expressed in the building's form and color. When I spoke about it in this way, it was understood. And then this fellow told me something very interesting; he said that he had asked because everything in Japan is made in white and gray, and he wasn't used to seeing a colored building. I thought about that and I thought about all the Japanese temples and the richness of colors in the rice paper and the painted walls and the wood and the stone bases and the colors of the landscapes. I have to admit that I was really surprised. They have obviously been so conditioned by modern architecture that most things – buildings in particular – are all made in white and gray. They are silvery. (As an aside, this is a country where 80% of the automobiles are white. I heard that they've just instituted a new law for the automobile makers to produce equal numbers of cars in other colors, so as to reduce the monotony of the auto landscape.)

Western symbol systems, when imported to Japan, may not always work, but I think that we've had very good experiences with them, especially with the colors we've used. I believe color is one of the reasons that our Japanese clients keep coming back to us. It's the color, the question of color. Once they understand they say, *"but of course"*.

We understand that we're not building temples; we can't use Japanese landscape or color symbolism. So we must introduce another system. Symbols and ideas have long been traded back and forth across cultural and political borders; both in the East, and the West. I'm rather confident you would find that the majority of buildings already built or being constructed in Japan today are no closer to the mark in carrying on the ancient traditions of temple building than are the importations done by myself and other Western architects. Similarities and differences are necessary and will always prevail.

Alongside the jewelry, lighting, packaging, furniture, tableware, etc. that you have designed, it is, in particular, your work for the stage that has attracted attention. Is it really true that you design stage sets and even costumes?

Yes it's true that I have and I would do it again. It really isn't so unusual for an architect to be involved in designing for the theater. Throughout the history of stage and scenographic design you can find a number of architects and artists. In the Renaissance and Baroque eras, there was Navarre, and in the early Modern age there was Oskar Schlemmer with his work at the Bauhaus. Matisse made costumes for the church. David Douglas, in his photos of Picasso's studio, shows us how the artist was constantly making cardboard objects and propping them up from the back with little supports. *The Bathers* exhibits a scenographic understanding of the stage as much as it does an understanding of sculpture. You can see it in terms of a series of flat planes that have been made graphic and therefore appropriate to the stage. The contemporary painter David Hockney has understood *The Bathers* in this way, and reinterpreted it in his art. One of my difficulties with Martha Graham's choreography is that although it is abstract and never quite real, it seeks to imitate a kind of reality that people like Picasso, Matisse and Hockney always understood as theater. The imagination is piqued by a mere suggestion. You don't try to make the rock real, but you

draw the rock. Through drawing, an expression of the thing and its space emerges. The stage is the perfect place to exercise your interests in these characteristics of space.

Theater, in order to exist, must take place in an essentially public domain. It's why I find this work so compelling. It is both spectacle and ritual with a purpose, an audience. The interesting question is not why you are doing it, but rather how it will be done. For me, it's quite natural for architects to be engaged in these kinds of activities.

None of your clients for product design manufacture anonymous mass products. Would you decline to work for a mass producer?

No, I don't think I would decline.

We know who designed the "Volkswagen". We know who designed the "Miata". The person who designed the "Miata" is not a household name but he is well known in the field of automobile design. One of the reasons that I am hired or that people like me are hired is that our names are used as part of the marketing of the objects we design. However, I think this is probably a time when we are all feeling the effects of the superficial endorsement and other ways of capitalizing on someone else's talent. For example, a basketball player, a designer or a political figure, a person who is either recognized as an authority or respected for his integrity, holds up a plate and advertises it in a national magazine. You think, well, he's well known for one thing, he's endorsing this other thing. I always look for a connection between the two. When Michael Jordan advertises athletic shoes he's obviously getting paid for it, but it's also a part of his profession. If I endorse a kitchen product it's because of its design and its quality and because I specify it in my buildings. So there's a connection. It troubles me when I can't find the strand that ties it all together. It starts with blue jeans and ends with tea kettles.

I don't think I've ever been asked to do something anonymously. I was once invited, along with Giorgio Armani, to do a "designer" telephone for Italtel in Italy. They wanted me to design a phone that they would make and hype in various ways. What's curious is that at the same time they were making an everyday phone as well, a phone that they decided should be designed by committee. I suggested that we combine the "designer" phone with the "everyday" model and make one good telephone. They were quite surprised that I would be willing to do that, yet at the same time it was such a foreign thought to me that there was to be such a difference between one phone and another. Although they were quite taken with the idea, the project as a whole died on account of a change in the direction of the company. I wish it hadn't, because whether my name would have been used or not, to have my telephone in every house in Italy sounded pretty interesting.

What does the Michael Graves design process consist of?

Just as I do in architecture, I find out what the boundaries of the project are; what you can and can't do. Once you know that, you know pretty well how you can break the rules. For example, a context for a building site can be both a piece of land bounded by two streets and a stream or it can be the width of a flame on a kitchen stove. You wonder about how the building and the kettle will fit into their respective contexts. You make yourself believe that the context was never an issue, and that it's absolutely natural for your project to fit within these materials or dimensions.

You always want to know all of the boundaries of a project, from materials to budget to its history as an object. Obviously, making a museum is different from making a parking garage. Similarly, designing a chair is different from designing a tea service. Historical precedent is important to me; I want to make continuities. Not that what you make is like the one before, but that you can perceive its ancestors. I find it interesting that each time we start a project for Alessi, they supply us with its complete history, as they and other manufacturers have produced it; a range of what this object has been. If it is part of a group of objects then it takes on the characteristics of an ensemble. It becomes, as Alessi says, part of the "family". It's always interesting to start new families because not all kitchens are the same. They need different kinds of expression and different personalities. So to start a project you have materials, a program, and issues of context and family. Design is, in a sense, breaking or bending the rules, so that the result is something which is familiar, yet new. It might even make you think about the object in a different way.

What role is played by your staff? Do you even have time to think, given the tasks of managing such a large studio as yours?

This is a good question. I made a decision a long time ago that if I could have a variety of projects, from architecture to interiors to furniture, fabrics and objects that enliven the interiors – life would be more interesting than if I were just doing one thing. Having made that decision, the only practical way to manage it was to have a staff large enough and talented enough so that all those activities could go on at the same time. Working in this way is not linear - there is a simultaneity involved. I can't stop all building activities while I'm designing a chair and reviewing its proto-types. From architecture to artifacts, we are constantly working together. If you were to pluralize "Michael Graves, Architect" to "Michael Graves, *Architects*", I would be happy about it. There are people in our office who have very good ideas, and who are quite able not only to follow through on instructions, but to add their own inventions along the way. Yes, it's true that I set the character

for every project, but its development is very much a team project. Administration, since I am not a skilled administrator, is taken care of by very gifted people, some of them architects, some of them not. The legal work is done by people who do that sort of thing, just as the technical part of building design is taken care of by people talented and interested in that aspect of architecture. No single area is more important than another in our office; you don't find the technicians on a differ-ent floor or in a different building, as you might in other places. That's because every technical question is also a design question and every design question has technical ramifications, whether it's a butter dish or a building.

I remember reading once that a society or culture could be defined in part as a sharing of respons-ibilities between individuals. Think of an early farmer. He has to tend his crops, something at which he happens to be very skilled, he makes his clothing, builds his house. He does everything by himself, for himself. But one day he meets someone who has become much better at building houses. They benefit mutually if they share their skills. That bartering and sharing and trading is really what makes a dependence on each other so interesting, and in a way it's what gives us our cities. There are some things that I do better than others, as all of us do. There are some things I prefer to do over other things too. I suppose the rub comes when you prefer to do things at which you're not very good. Isn't that too often the case!

Are there any changes that you envision having an impact on your work in the next few years?

I think that there have already been two big changes that have clearly affected the way we work and the work that we do. One of them concerns the number and variety of objects we have produced so far. We presently have enough of an assortment of pieces to put them all together into one space and offer them as a collection – from furniture to fabrics, to articles for the table. Because of this we have the opportunity to see these things in ways that were impossible before. We can observe similarities and differences and connections, and we can begin to understand more clearly how these things all work together. Fifteen years ago this would not have been conceivable, as we had only designed a few fabrics and some pieces of furniture; certainly not as much as we have now. The other change relates to the fact that we have a collection of pieces. Today, we're more frequently contacted by companies which ask us to work on consumer goods. Ten years ago, Thompson Consumer Electronics may have been interested in us for designing their buildings, but now, they are interested in having us design products as well. So far we've only had discussions about these things – telephones and televisions – both of which would be fascinating to pursue. We'll see where it goes. I may find that ultimately there is little to no room to design, or rather "break the rules", of the object. It is also possible that they might not hold enough interest for us. There are certain things I would not want to do because I think that they require a more specialized expertise. Cars for instance; they're one of those specialties that require a very particular type of training, as well as your full attention. I'm neither qualified nor willing to do that, although I would love to.

What is the design look of the near future? How will things look in design as a whole? What effect will the Pacific Rim have?

I think things are pretty cross-cultural already, so I doubt that an influence like the Pacific Rim will have much effect on the way we conceive of design. However, I do believe that things won't be seen as singularly as Black Matte or Porsche Design were in the Eighties. Actually, what will happen I think – and this is from someone who never makes predictions – is that there will be black and there will be white and everything in between, as well as a greater variety of color. For example, we recently designed a watch that we thought was interesting on its own terms. We thought that it would be something people would like. We've now been asked to design the same watch in color, many colors, but specifically for Italy. Here we had thought we had designed this "good for all people all times" watch and the response is "yes, but can you do it in many colors, each with its

own character". On the one hand you wonder, *"why should we bother"*, but on the other hand, *"why not, it's something we hadn't considered"*. The sensibility of Italy is that objects should be individualized. A watch is more or less anonymous, but for a special market it is given another personality. It makes me think that variety will be the spice of life. Who knows, in addition to variety in color, there could be just as many takes on tradition or on modernism. Overall though, I suppose that I would prefer to see things settle down and display a greater consensus.

Between your practice and your academic responsibilities, you must lead a very busy life. How do you manage to unwind from work?

The biggest issue for me is trying to rid myself of the guilt – the guilt of being away from the office, of not working. I'm always looking for ways to get something done so I can feel like I'm able to take the night off, or the weekend off or something like that. It's important for people who are busy to clarify things so that they can say to themselves, *"I need a break. Tomorrow is the day I'll think about work, when I'm at the office."* You've got to find a way to enjoy yourself. That's something that's actually new to me. I have to reinforce the time that's offered and make it count

for as much as it can. I know I could make my life simpler in a number of ways – hiring more help for instance, but I don't want to give up my privacy. I don't want somebody here in the kitchen, fixing the tea for us. I want to be able to walk around and do what I want to do. Perhaps people who have had help all their lives don't notice the intrusion. I've never lived that way so I expect that I wouldn't be able to adjust. There are a lot of things I do, like laundry, that someone else could certainly do, but there's a great sense of accomplishment I get from taking the time to do these everyday sorts of things. For instance, I love being in the yard – and I love raking – Zen raking I call it – though I don't especially like weeding. After twenty years of working on my house and its garden, I find it really wonderful to be able to look out the window in the morning and just watch the sun move across the walls. At that moment you have to say that maybe it is all worth it.

I'm reminded of a Robert Motherwell interview I read a number of years ago. He was being asked about how he spent his weekends. He replied that he always spent them the same way, and it was better that people didn't know what it was that he did. The interviewer kept asking and asking until Motherwell gave in. He said that what he did was look at books. Now by that he meant he was looking at art books. I mean he was looking – he needed to look at paintings. It was a great enjoyment for him; it is for me as well. Without guilt – just looking at books.

What would you most like to design someday? What task would most excite you as a designer?

The next opportunity? I've never really given it much thought, and I'm afraid that my answer might not be that interesting. I've been fortunate because I've gotten to do all the things that I've wanted to design, furniture and objects and so on. Of the kinds of things that we haven't done, I guess I would like to design bathroom fixtures, again, not too glamorous but, sinks and so on. It could be very interesting!

I suppose I would also like to design a line of hardware because what's available now is either too interesting or not interesting enough. By too interesting, I mean that somebody's tried too hard and has missed. We haven't been asked to do it, but we haven't sought it out either. I'd like to design hardware so I could use it in my own buildings. But in addition, I'd have to say that there's nothing quite as satisfying as seeing your work in somebody else's building.

The last time I was at the Metropolitan Museum of Art in New York, I happened to notice one of our ceiling fixtures had been used in a recent renovation. Someone had placed it up close to the ceiling, a way that it had never been intended to be installed. I had never seen it that way before – it looked great. It was good to see an old friend in a new context, a new interpretation. I have to say it made me smile.

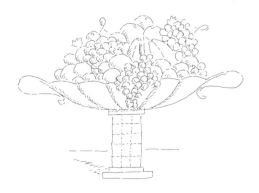

The interview was conducted by Sybil McKenna
in March 1994 in Princeton, New Jersey.

Rainer Krause

The "Graves Family" – Designs for the Set Table

In 1979, Alberto Alessi's "Tea & Coffee Piazza" project anticipated much of what would set the standard in the 1980s, the "Golden Age" of design. The idea of having a large number of architects and designers work on one and the same product according to certain specifications runs like a red thread through the 1980s and (nearly always) yielded a promising approach in the search for new design well into the 1990s. Alberto Alessi had himself not exactly expected the great success which his project was to have. He clearly regarded it more as an opportunity to shake off the old traditional shackles when it came to product development and to find entirely new approaches for the family business. His thirst for the adventure, which he slated by working together with major architects from Europe, America and Japan, most certainly also played a role that should not be underestimated – no mean achievement at a time when the age of the fax was still to dawn.

When Alessi presented the results of this four-year development process to the international public in 1983 under the new label "Officina Alessi", he not only set in mo-

Left
Kettle. Model for Alessi, 1985

Above
Still life, 1991

83

tion the new eclecticism that was to be one of the characteristic currents in design in the 1980s. For at the same time he also opened up a completely new field of activity for the eleven architects who were involved in the project.

For Italian architects, it had long been common practice – not least because of the dearth of building contracts in post-War Italy – to design everything, from silverware to lamps, to wall units. This is also the only explanation for the legend that has grown up around Italian design.

In other countries, on the other hand, a painstakingly fine distinction was usually drawn between architecture and design. Either you were an architect or you were a designer. From this point of view, it was certainly a great stroke of luck that none of the partners Alessi so hoped would work with him turned him down when he asked them to design a silver coffee and tea service. For, with the exception of Oscar Tusquets and Hans Hollein, all the others involved had little or no experience in design.

Left
Programma 6. Silver tea service for the Alessi Tea and Coffee Piazza collection, 1982

Right
Programma 6. Silver teapot for the Alessi Tea and Coffee Piazza collection, 1982

84

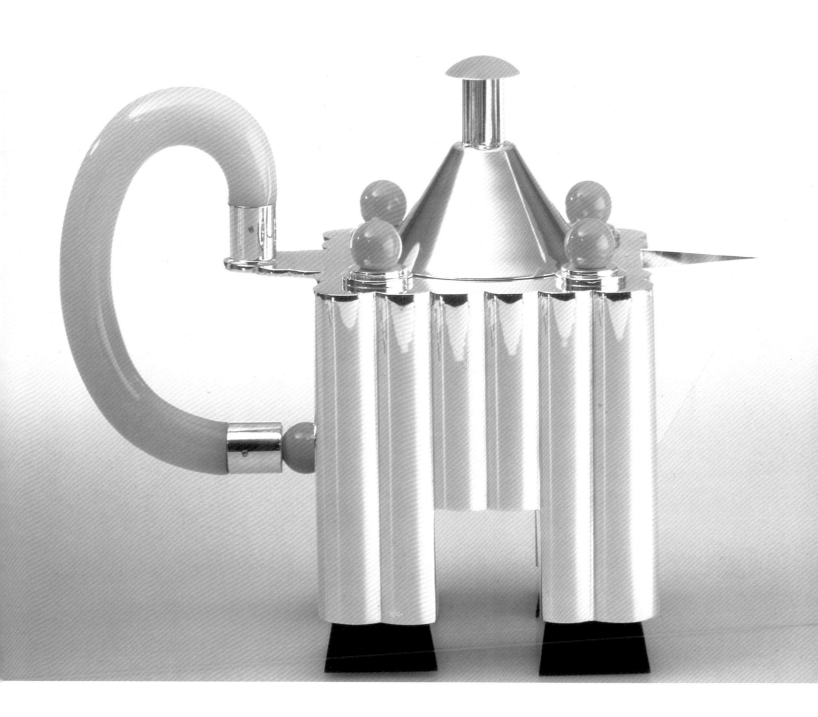

Michael Graves, whom Alessi regarded as the prime representative of American Post-Modernism, had at that point also done very little work in the field of design. He had admittedly created a large number of designs for the showrooms of Sunar, an American firm: from 1977 to 1981, for example, a chair with arm rests, an easy chair, a sofa and two tables. Indeed, these pieces were so well received that it was not long before they were being produced under license for Europe by the Milan furniture company Sawaya & Moroni and thus also became known in Europe as ostensibly Italian design. Yet apart from these initial dabblings, Graves had done no further design work proper. Thus, when Alberto Alessi, or so the latter narrates, approached Michael Graves, he immediately met with an enthusiastic response.

Left
Kettle for Alessi, 1985
Kettle studies, 1991

Right
Creamer and sugar bowl for Alessi, 1985
Kettle studies, 1991

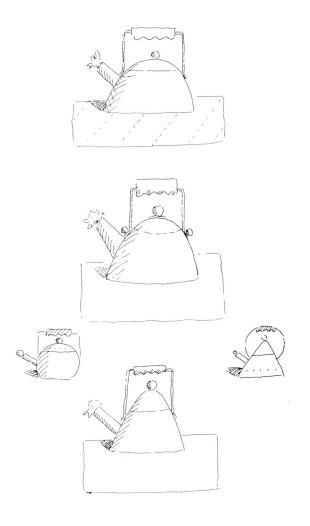

Michael Graves is an architect of great deeds. From the Newark Museum to salt and pepper shakers — his structures and designs encompass the unique quality of transcending time and function in our rapidly changing society. He is a true genius. Lucinda and I are very proud to have Michael Graves as a neighbor and friend. At the National Governors Association of 1992, hosted in Princeton, the First Ladies and other dignitaries had the unique opportunity to meet Michael Graves and enjoy a personal tour of his extraordinary home. We hope that his creative insights will continue to enrich the lives of the people of New Jersey and the nation.

Jim und
Lucinda Florio

Until 1994, Governor and First Lady of the State of New Jersey, USA

Graves' contribution to the "Tea & Coffee Piazza" was an inspired cross-section of his formal and stylistic canon and consisted of a six-piece service including a teapot and coffee pot, sugar bowl, milk jug, teaspoon and serving tray made of silver, aluminum, imitation ivory and Bakelite. This is truly "micro-architecture" for the table in the best sense of the term, as splendid and rich as his architectural language, a refined amalgam of Biedermeier, Wiener Werkstätte and Art Deco. Already famous for his use of color in architecture, Graves is a past master at using it in his designs. The imitation ivory softens the coldness of the fluted silver surfaces, the light-blue spheres and hemi-spheres made of aluminum diminish what would otherwise be an overly Classical con-trast between the silver bodies and the black Bakelite bases, imbuing the whole with a cheerfulness that is so typical of Graves' designs.

After this extremely successful start with Officina Alessi, in 1985 he landed his second big hit for Alessi's normal line of products. His kettle, the absolute icon of Post-Modern articles for everyday use, soon became an international bestseller. It is the American answer to Richard Sapper's European kettle (also designed for Alessi). Whereas Sapper's kettle meets or at least appears to meet all the criteria of "form fol-

From left to right
Pepper mill and salt shaker for Alessi, 1987

Coffee pot with press filter for Alessi, 1987

Ice-cube container for Alessi, 1992

Casserole, trays and forks for Alessi, 1992

Demi-cup with spoon for Alessi, 1988-9

lows function", the maxim of a famous colleague from Chicago, Graves' design shows that he is not overly interested in such matters. Whereas his silver tea and coffee set for Officina Alessi was a typical product for Sundays only, his flute kettle is intended as an object of everyday use. Richard Sapper hides the "melodic flute" in what appears to be the kettle's spout, whereas Graves highlights the function of the flute on the kettle by adding a red plastic bird to the spout. Metaphor becomes design. And the striking conical form ultimately not only makes the kettle so impressive but also ensures that it functions outstandingly well. The narrative design of his flute kettle enjoyed such an enormous success that, by the end of the 1980s, Graves was gradually able to expand his "Fun Design" into the "Graves Family".

In the meantime, for example, the colors and materials used in his kettle are to be encountered in a large number of other items of tableware: An initial addition were the milk jug and sugar bowl, both miniature versions of the famous kettle form. He comes up with an especially eye-catching solution with his saltcellars and pepperpots. As in the case of the kettle, it is the contrast of shiny high-grade steel and matted blue

Graves Family of products for Alessi, 1984-94

Measuring cups. Prototypes for Alessi, 1990

The Graves Design Collection is like no other. We are not aware of work by an American product designer that has the range, the excitement and the consistent high quality. It brings us great pleasure to present the entire collection to an appreciative and enthusiastic audience.

Oliver Andes,
Jeffrey Gilbert

Owners of The Archive Shop for product design, Easton, Pennsylvania

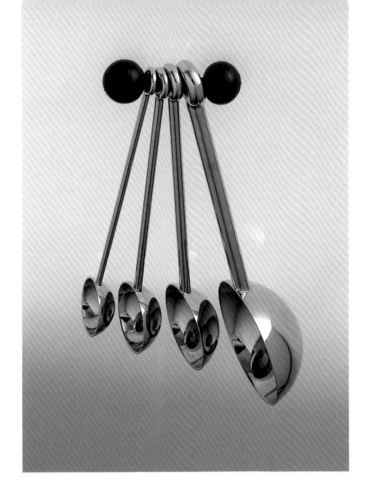

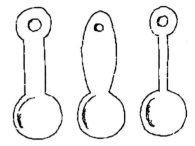

plastic that catches the eye; again, to an even greater degree than the kettle, both objects are miniature works of architecture for the table. The salt cellar looks like the turret of a castle and the pepperpot resembles the turret from a cartoon, an initial anticipation of his designs for The Walt Disney Company.

The latest members of the Graves Family, a pressfilter coffeepot, cups and a butter dish, reveal design elements characteristic of his great role model, Josef Hoffmann. More than any other architect, Hoffmann has had a major, enduring influence on Michael Graves, precisely in the field of design. It is therefore hardly surprising if Graves repeatedly makes use of furniture and other objects Hoffmann designed in his own interiors. In the dining room he designed for the Sanders family in Princeton, New Jersey, Graves introduced Hoffmann's famous "Patrician" glasses, which are still being produced by the Lobmeyr firm in Vienna today. The silver centerpiece by Graves also alludes to a form that was repeatedly varied by Hoffmann for the Wiener Werkstätte; together with the cutlery and plates designed by Graves, the result is thus a tremendously rich table setting which does not look as if it were an amalgam of master and pupil, of the Old and New Worlds.

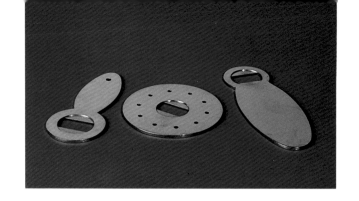

Left
Measuring spoons. Prototypes for Alessi, 1990

Design sketches for measuring spoons for Alessi, 1990

Right
Bottle openers. Prototypes for Alessi, 1993

Flatware for Alessi, 1994

Sitting in that small room filled with books over the Chinese restaurant during those late night charettes, all I can remember now is sharpening all those Prisma color pencils over and over and over, and thinking to myself how critical it was to observe and not participate.

Little did I know, years later, what an effect observing those hours of tedious drafting and sketching would have on my life.

He was and will always remain my teacher.

Peter Arnell

One of Michael Graves first assistants, now head of the Arnell Bickford Associates advertising agency in New York, New York

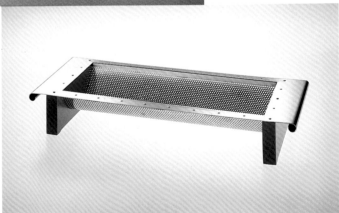

In 1984, the young American design company Swid Powell, its attention having been caught by Alessi's successes, also asked Michael Graves and some European architects to design a set of tableware. Although in this case – unlike the "Tea & Coffee Piazza" by Alessi – it was only a matter of designing two-dimensional decorations, the result Graves came up with was a tremendously attractive collection of designs, some of which have such an original impact on the basic shape that they appear to transform the very porcelain. "Delos" and "Corinth", the two designs for dinnerware Graves created for this collection, go back to Classical and Neo-Classical uses of form and color. The "Corinth" design stands out for its stylized plant motifs in restrained, elegant hues of gray, and white which refine the simple underlying porcelain forms. By contrast, the "Delos" plates with their strong red and blues so typical of Graves' work are strikingly impressive and sumptuous. With "Delos", Graves concentrated the design on the broad rim of the plate, leaving only traces of decoration to fade out toward the center of the plate. In the design for "Corinth" he went decidedly further and covered the entire bottom of the plate with a star motif which conjures up strong associations with the famous stage sets of the young Karl Friedrich Schinkel for Mozart's "Magic Flute".

From left to right
Cruet stands and sugar caster for Alessi, 1994

Bread basket for Alessi, 1994

Timekeeper for Alessi, 1992

Kitchen clock for Alessi, 1991

In the third design for Swid Powell, Graves not only designed the ornamentation but the object as a whole: His famous "Big Dripper" from the year 1986 is a truly complex product in which the iconography of everyday culture coincides with the color symbolism so characteristic of Graves' work, conjuring up a cheerfully ironic but at the same time magnificent interplay of forms. There is probably hardly a more refined variation on the traditional coffee-filter than Michael Graves' "Big Dripper"; in no other work is the cylindrical coffee filter attachment so coherently integrated into the actual coffee pot. Once the coffee has dripped through, the filter is removed, the lid is replaced, and the pot restored to its original spherical shape.

Were it not for the Pompeian red of the cross-shaped base, the greenish wavy lines signaling liquid and the gold forming the rim on the filter attachment (a gold-rimmed

Left
Corinth porcelain dinnerware for Swid Powell, 1986-7

Right
Delos plate for Swid Powell, 1986-7

Corinth porcelain dinnerware for Swid Powell, 1986-7

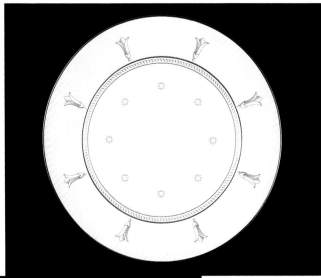

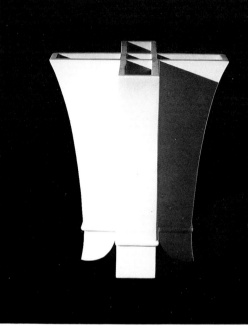

filter!) and on the knob of the lid, one would be tempted to speak in terms of a
thoroughly functionalistic design. However, the use of color is unsettling; it renders
the use of function and content deeply ironic while at the same time being amusing.
In no other Graves' design for the table does color play such an important role, in no
other work does the predominantly decorative element of color so greatly alter the
statement of an object. It is as if Graves chose such an "earth-shaking" thing as a
Melitta coffee pot to demonstrate that he is perfectly at home as a designer. Yet he
also puts this capability into question by seeming to go over the top with the use of
color and the application of magnificent detail in his "Big Dripper". As in the case of
Alessi's water kettle, the "Big Dripper" for Swid Powell is not found exclusively in the
kitchen, respectively on the table. Borrowing from the notion of the spherical coffee
pot as mother, there are two baby-spheres for the sugar and the milk, rounding out

From left to right
Salad servers for Swid Powell, 1990

Vase. Model for Swid Powell, 1987

Design sketches for vases, 1986

Vases for Swid Powell, 1989

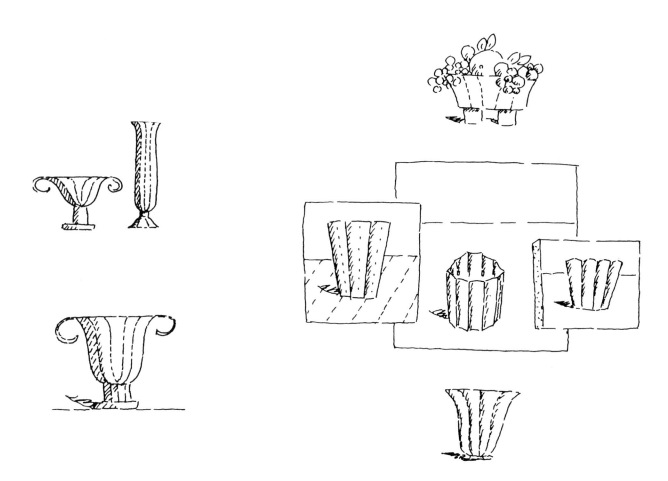

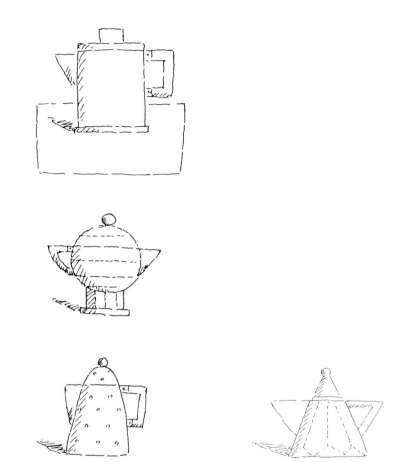

the ensemble, which looks like an everyday object but was surely designed with Sunday-best in mind. Precisely in the design of his more elaborate pieces, Michael Graves loves to evoke, as he did in the objects for Alessi and Swid Powell, the periods he most prefers – Classical Rome, Viennese Biedermeier and Neo-Classicism.

In 1986, he designed a limited series of centerpieces (trays, fruit bowls and vases) for Steuben, the American glass manufacturers. He called them "Archaic Vessels", whereby the title is also the underlying program he pursues. These lead crystal bowls and vases on filigree bronze structures, designed by Graves with great sensitivity and inspired by Etruscan designs, represent important elements linking the world of inanimate objects (furniture, etc.) and the living world (flowers and fruit). It is regrettable that these works, which are so indebted to Europe, are not also marketed there.

In 1987, WMF, a German company, persuaded Graves to design a few silver objects for them. Unfortunately, however, only a champagne-cooler actually went into

Above
Big Dripper. Coffee pot, sugar bowl and creamer for Swid Powell, 1986-7

Below
Big Dripper. Coffee pot with filter for Swid Powell, 1986-7

101

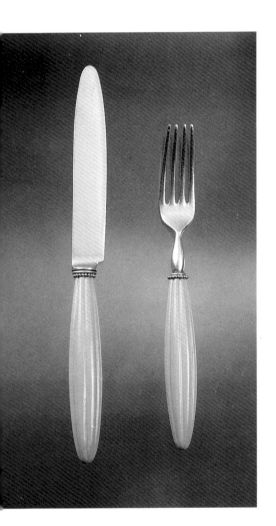

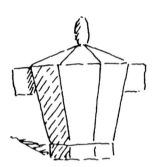

production. The conical silver container rests, in true Biedermeier style, on a round black wooden base. Even the fluted handles made of imitation ivory (he had already used the same design for a set of cutlery that was created the same year but never got beyond the prototype stage) draw on the formal language of the Viennese Biedermeier, which are as important for Graves as the Wiener Werkstätte and their initiator Josef Hoffmann. Signs of the latter's influence on Graves' designs are particularly evident in the two elaborate cups he created.

In 1982, Graves designed a cup for the *Gentlemen's Quarterly Magazine* made of such diverse material as imitation marble, high-grade steel, bird's eye maple and ebony. The base and actual cup are still strongly reminiscent of Graves' approach to form in his furniture designs for Sunar, although the elegant handles are quite obviously references to the "Rococo Phase" of Josef Hoffmann's work. The "Samuel C. Miller Cup", designed five years later for the Newark Museum (and produced by Tiffany's in New Jersey), also attests to Graves' admiration for the Viennese architect's great imaginativeness.

From left to right
Silverware. Prototype for Sasaki, 1987

Design sketches for the ice-cube container by Cleto Munari, 1988

Champagne cooler for WMF, 1987

Ice-cube container for Cleto Munari, 1988

Whenever Michael visits the shop, he unfailingly zeroes in on an object or piece of furniture with the cleanest sense of proportion and design. The simple lines of Biedermeier, particularily hose examples of North German furniture made in Berlin, are pure reductions of architecture in themselves. It makes sense that these pieces have the strongest appeal. As a designer, Michael expresses a similar clarity of thought in his coffee set and kettle pieces. Whether architectural or utilitarian, Michael s sensibilities perfect the pure and simple and are, I find, incredibly inspiring.

Niall Smith

Antique dealer in New York,
New York

From left to right
**Archaic Vessel. Fruit bowl for Steuben Glass,
1986-8**

**Archaic Vessels. Design sketches for a flower
vase for Steuben Glass, 1986**

**Archaic Vessels. Design sketches for bowls for
Steuben Glass, 1986**

**Archaic Vessel. Flower vase for Steuben Glass,
1986-8**

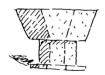 

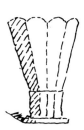  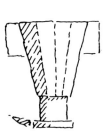

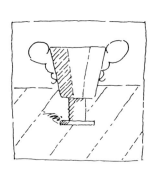 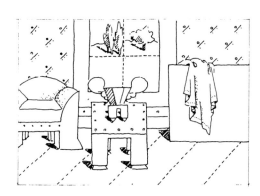 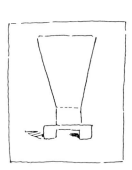

From left to right

**Design sketches for the Gentlemen s Quarterly
Manstyle Award, 1982**

**Samuel C. Miller Cup. Silver cup for Samuel
C. Miller s 20th anniversary as director of the
Newark Museum, Tiffany & Co., New York,
New York, 1987**

**Gentlemen s Quarterly Manstyle Award. Cup
for the Gentlemen s Quarterly periodical, 1982**

Delta Society Benefit Biscuit Box , 1993

From left to right

Tableware. Prototype for The Walt Disney Company, 1992

Tableware for The Walt Disney World Swan Hotel, Orlando, Florida, 1988

Mickey kettle. Model for The Walt Disney Company, 1992-3

108

In contrast to these elaborate designs, most of which were manufactured only as individual items and are accessible only to few, Graves' most recent work will reach the public at large.

For the two hotels he designed for Disney World, Graves not only created a number of pieces of furniture but also several designs for the tableware of the various restaurants. Whereas the plate decorations for Swid Powell were more in a Classical/Neo-Classical vein, as was foreseen in the contractual specifications, the very different tableware designs for the Disney World hotels have an emphatically popular character. The broad spectrum of motifs (which usually refer to the names of the respective restaurants) ranges from oversized, naturalistically drawn orange slices to allusions to historical events and cheerfully distractive decorations. It is proof of Graves' wealth of ideas

in the development of interior design, his mastery as a draftsman and his great talent of taking the environment surrounding the tasks he is commissioned to accomplish into account in a convincing and coherent manner.

The "Mickey" kettle (and there is, again, an accompanying creamer and sugar bowl), which was launched on the market in fall 1993, is, for the time being, the pinnacle of Graves' design œuvre, which is relatively small in relation to his architectural output. Graves' "Mickey" kettle designed for Disney appears to be based on the flute kettle for Alessi, but on closer examination one finds that the only thing the two designs have in common is the typology. Whereas the Alessi kettle exhibits definite architectural references, the round shape of the body of the "Mickey" kettle with its Mickey Mouse-shaped handle is a comic strip that has been turned into a design. In contrast to most of Graves' other designs with their many cultural references, this kettle is a product with a message that is readily understandable to everyone. It is a souvenir of the excursion into a (commercially oriented) fantasy world: Disney World, and yet at the same time a practical everyday product.

From left to right

Porcelain service for the dining room of the Crown American administration building, 1986-8

Design drawing for the Martini glass for Bombay Sapphire Gin, 1991

Martini glass for Bombay Sapphire Gin, 1991

Bathroom collection. Prototypes for Markuse, 1993

Candleholder for Architectural Products, 1992

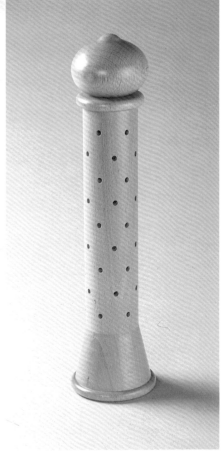

As in the case of this most recent product, Michael Graves has never been averse in any of his other designs for tableware to uniting seemingly irreconcilable opposites in one product. In the field of tension between past and present, between highbrow art and everyday culture, between Europe and America, he has, since 1979, been developing a new product language. It was somewhat over-hastily classified as "Post-Modern" but in reality goes far beyond, leaving Post-Modernism well behind it. The products he has created in this fashion are not only convincing as functional examples of Post-Modernist design but in a variety of other respects. For with their unique mixture of functionality, elegance, poetry and intense color, Michael Graves' objects differ fundamentally from those of other contemporary designers. It is this which makes them products that we will still enjoy using many years from now.

The barn on our farm is an oasis, a retreat, a Michael Graves Creation. It blends our life style with his unique designs, silos, haylofts, stalls, clocks, beds, peppermills, tea kettles, mailboxes.

Susan and Donald Newhouse

Clients of Michael Graves, New Jersey

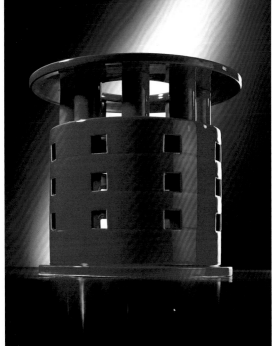

From left to right

Tray for Twergi, 1991

Pepper mill for Twergi, 1991

Ikon Bowls. Fruit bowls for Waechtersbacher Keramik, Germany, 1991

Design drawing for fruit bowl for Waechtersbacher Keramik, 1991

Graves charm bracelet. Designed for
Belvedere Studio, 1991

Janet Abrams

"Gesamtkunstwerk" – Coming Home to Rome

When I first met Michael Graves he was working from an office on Witherspoon Street in Princeton, in a kind of attic above a Chinese restaurant. It was 1982, and I'd flown to the States to interview the "New York Five", find out where they'd each got to, ten years on. Eisenman/Graves/Gwathmey/Hejduk/Meier: their names were like a mantra. Everybody knew about the "white" architects; the lucky ones even owned a copy of *Five Architects*, the bible of their becoming. I've forgotten exactly what we talked about though I distinctly recall spilling tea down my suit out of sheer nervousness five minutes before Michael entered the conference room. There was a long, possibly staged, interlude during the interview when he took a phone call from fellow-Fiver Peter Eisenman; they are still close buddies even if, by now, aesthetically, further apart than ever. I also recall the atmosphere of the office, the little painted collages that seemed to lurk on the tops of plan chests, the *homely* quality of the space, which was a true atelier, and quite unlike most architects' offices I'd visited thus far.

Left
The Warehouse. Michael Graves residence in Princeton, New Jersey, 1986

Right
The Warehouse. Bedroom in the Michael Graves residence, 1986

Graves was in the ascendant. Already known for a number of neo-Corbusian domestic projects in the Princeton vicinity, and "paper projects" like the Fargo-Moorhead Cultural Bridge, he had leapt to attention with the Portland Public Office building, completed in 1982. Its defiantly decorative elevations fired the opening shot in the Great Facade Wars, and the building (which played a cameo role in the movie *Body of Evidence*, 1992) was claimed as the harbinger of Post-Modernism in architecture. Eleven years later, he is a household name – a rare achievement for an architect anywhere – and the Graves portfolio encompasses buildings in America, Europe and Japan, plus a wide array of designs from interior furnishings to items of personal adornment. Today, the entire operation (the architecture studio and the affiliated Graves Design) occupies an atmospheric building at 341 Nassau Street, Princeton's leafy main artery, some fifteen minutes' walk east of the Ivy League university campus where Graves has taught for over thirty years.

A designer's own living and work spaces are usually indicative of their personality and design persuasion; in Graves's case, his home and studio are open books of an intense aesthetic sensibility. Where Witherspoon Street was a cozy warren, 341 Nassau Street is a maze, with scuffed flights of wooden stairs and narrow passageways leading up, down, around, and through the many levels of this distinctly un-corporate headquarters. Cased models of recent architecture projects line the walls, prototypes are stacked in the bustling product-design studio and – adding to the atmosphere of a creative menagerie – Graves' dog is usually to be found padding the hallways. A small building across the street has recently been annexed as a "studio store" (taking cues from one of Graves's best-known clients, The Walt Disney Company), and a branch office is maintained in New York.

For me, the key to all of Michael's work, from skyscrapers to teapots, is his house, a work in progress that he has been refining for nearly twenty years. It is the house of a collector, of one devoted to the pursuit of the object of beauty. I believe that his ideal vision of this house is that of a microcosm of a civilized world in which every object, every building, and life itself, is a thing of beauty. This philosophy may not be fashionable in our fragmented and deconstructed world today, but I have always admired what I believe to be Michael's unwavering devotion to it.

Pilar Viladas

Journalist for architecture and interior design in Los Angeles, California

Though separate domains, Graves' office and his own home, just around the corner,
form a kind of workplace/residence continuum which reminds one of a Palladian agri-
cultural estate. Over the years, he has used his house as a practical laboratory for his
own architectural development, much as Frank Lloyd Wright did in his studio-home
in Oak Park, or as Frank Gehry has done in Santa Monica. Documented in Graves'
first Rizzoli monograph as the anonymous "Warehouse, Princeton", but identified in
the subsequent volume as the architect's own residence, the house and its grounds
have undergone gradual transformation from a simple L-shaped warehouse (built by
Italian stonemasons who were imported to work on the university buildings) to what
is by now a veritable stately home.

A demonstration not only of Graves's taste in architecture and landscape, it is also a setting for his own domestic artifacts: light fittings, clocks, picture frames, bowls, chairs, are resplendently arrayed in this ultimate "show home", a walk-through catalogue of his aesthetic. One is reminded of the Ralph Lauren Polo store on Madison Avenue – a palazzo of consumption, decorated and trimmed with all sorts of authentic knick-knacks – except that in this case, it really is a *home* – the dog hair on a rumpled white-covered arm chair in one guest bedroom a rare lapse in perfection, testifying to actual use.

If a detective came to the Graves residence and wanted to know what kind of a man had lived there, I would point to just two sets of things. Not the neo-classical paintings, nor the piles of illustrated books on landscape and architecture, nor the fine library with tall shelves reaching towards a skylight, nor the Etruscan pots secreted in high niches like the cherished trophies of some latter-day Soane. No, I would choose the following clues: the collection of souvenir Tempiettos, and the set of antique magnifying glasses. Here, condensed as if dream motifs, are architecture and optical illusion, the miniature and the magnified, the distortions of history and the play of scale. Graves's chief preoccupations, in talismanic form.

From left to right

The Warehouse. Library in the Michael Graves residence in Princeton, New Jersey, 1986

The Warehouse. Michael Graves' library – Inkwell Collection

The Warehouse. Study in the Michael Graves residence, 1986

The house, as it has gradually matured, is like a slow-evolving Polaroid of one man's passion for Classicism. It is the coming into focus of an Italy of the imagination – the place which Graves continues to paint in his "Archaic Landscapes", whence he derives the criss-crossed tunics of his costume designs, the chiseled letter forms of his graphics, the heavy medallion-like shapes of his recent jewelry.

It is obvious that the formative experience of Graves's career was the time spent in Rome, from 1960 to 1962, as a Fellow of the American Academy. For a young man from the mid-West, who had never previously traveled to Europe, landing in Rome was an utter revelation. Until then he had had very little exposure to the history of architecture. "I had one history course in six years at Cincinnati, the last term of my senior year: the Greeks, the Romans to the Byzantines." A course with Siegfried Giedion at Harvard on Swedish Town Planning sticks in his mind – "buildings that

Loving Cup. Bracelet and earrings for Belvedere Studio, 1991

Landscape Cuff. Wristband/bracelet for Belvedere Studio, 1991

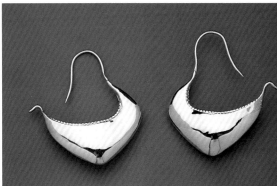

looked like keyholes". But overall, "it was an anti-intellectual time, a *doing* time. We talked about architecture in terms of keeping the rain out. We had a very curious idea of what architecture was." Arriving in Rome was bound to make a deep impression, and Graves spent his time drawing Borromini, selling his drawings to fund travel around the country. "I went everywhere. We'd get up and decide on an itinerary for the day, like, 'Today we will see round churches with wall paintings.' I can hardly believe how much time we had."

While Rome was pivotal to his subsequent career, Graves also acknowledges some influences back home in America. He jokes that "I'm the one architect that didn't work for anybody important, but I worked for wonderful people." A short stint at the office of Walter Gropius ("about one and a half minutes, actually working for somebody third in command doing Baghdad University") counted for less than the year he spent at the office of the multi-faceted designer George Nelson, after taking his Master's degree at Harvard. Trained as an architect and a Rome Prize Fellow himself, Nelson was also a writer, photographer, graphic designer, furniture designer, and editor of *Architectural Forum*, then the most important design magazine in America.

Left
Rings for Cleto Munari, 1985

Right
Watches for Markuse produced by Pierre Junod, 1992

Watch for Cleto Munari, 1985

The range of Nelson's activities (which included film titles and product packaging alongside his better-known seating) seems to have been a lasting inspiration. It was during this period, just prior to his departure for Rome, that Graves became familiar with the work of Charles Eames and textile designer Alexander Girard, who were also working as design consultants for Herman Miller. Girard's palette, influenced by the Native American culture of the South-West, remained a powerful source for Graves' own use of color.

The General Motors Tech Center, designed by the Saarinens, *père et fils,* was also an "extremely important" influence. Completed in 1956, in the heyday of pink Cadillacs and tail fins, the Detroit research campus of the giant auto manufacturer was a dramatic example of corporate Modernism: an arrangement of spartan Miesian pavilions, enlivened by vibrant color on certain elevations, giving them what Graves calls "already an adjectival, decorative look". He likens their simple colorful exuberance to the work of the Mexican architect Luis Barragan. "I remember going to the GM Tech Center when I was 17, when they had just opened – it was hard to see Modern buildings growing up in a backwater like Cincinnati. I walked into the Information Center, and there was a blonde in a white dress sitting at a round white desk, and behind her, a staircase going up with no visible means of support except some very thin metal struts." The totality of the *mis-en-scène*, what one might call the designed artifice, made a deep impression. "We did aspire to put ourselves into our buildings in that way."

Graves has always cared deeply about his own surroundings, and talks with equally fond recollection of arranging his home in Cincinnati, his studio at the American Academy, or his apartment on Bank Street in New York. As a young married student in the six-year architecture program at Cincinnati in the 1950s, ("in those days," he recalls, with a wry smile "you had to get married to get laid") many of his classmates were setting up households, and confronted the shortage of well-designed domestic artifacts. So they improvised, making their own furniture such as tables and TV cabinets – the device was then new. They went window-shopping at the local Good

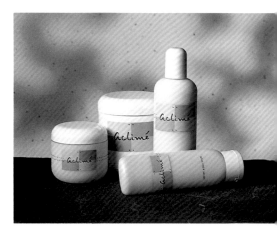

From left to right
Telephone. Prototype for Italtel, 1988

Corporate identity and packaging for Aclimé, 1991

125

Design Store which carried items approved by the Museum of Modern Art, and even drove up to the Herman Miller headquarters in Zeeland, Michigan, to buy Charles Eames furniture.

Consciously emulating Eames, whose artful photographs certainly contributed to the mystique of his designs, Graves made his own photographic compositions – Eames' "House of Cards" placed on a table, plants hanging, the light falling just so. Early in his career, Graves was asked to show examples of interiors he had done, having been recommended for a commission to design a house. Lacking a portfolio of interior design work, he swiftly put together some forty still life photographs of his own house.

Ten years ago, when Princeton Architectural Press was literally a one-man operation head-quartered on the back porch of my grad-student house, Michael Graves proposed that I publish the sequel to his highly successful monograph, *Buildings and Projects 1965-1981*. This astonished me then, and does even now.

An architect of international renown who had already published with the then most prestigious architectural press, stood little to gain – and presumably much to lose – by publishing with a yet-unproven student venture. As it turned out, Michael's confidence was not misplaced. Working closely with his office, we produced a book which far exceeded in scope and ambition anything we had done before. *Buildings and Projects 1982-1989* quickly became the best-selling book we have ever published. More important, it put Princeton Architectural Press on the map by demonstrating our ability to produce a monograph which rivaled (or exceeded) anything our competition had put together.

Michael's decision to publish with Princeton Architectural Press in our infancy was an act of extraordinary generosity for which I will always be grateful.

Kevin Lippert

Publisher, founder and owner of Princeton Architectural Press, New York, New York

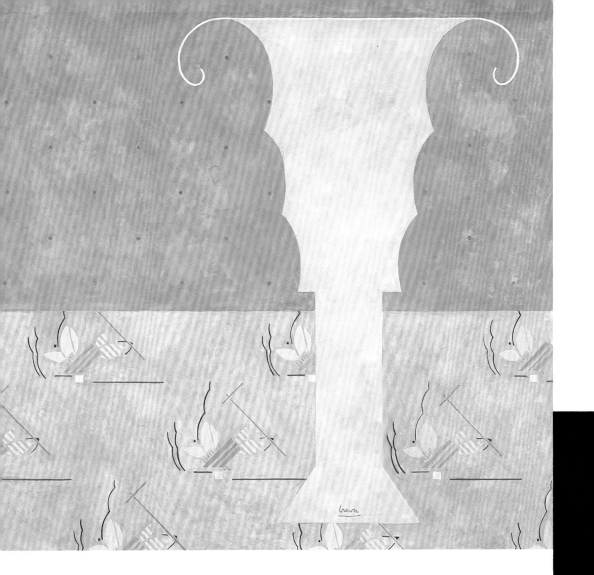

He arranged flatware, plants, furniture, and the one Etruscan vase which he then owned (bought in a flea market in Rome during his Fellowship years), shooting them "all very close-up because if you showed any more you'd see the background. It was all stage-setting." He got the job.

If the range of choice was limited when Graves was a student, he finds the anonymity of much contemporary product design just as dismaying. "Whether you go to Pottery Barn, Conran's or Tiffany's, it seems to me the level of personality is missing. The design has been watered down." His admiration for Eames, Nelson or earlier heroes, such as Josef Hoffmann of the Wiener Werkstätte, is based on a sense that "there's somebody home. There's talent, there's some *body* in the work". But the ideological distance between Graves design and the mainstream of contemporary product designers is striking. (He claims to have "no relation whatsoever" to the product design community. "It's really just like architecture ... it has its own little club.")

From left to right
Leather goods collection for Spinneyback, 1990-1
Illustration for Bloomingdale's shopping bag, 1982
Shopping bag for Bloomingdale's, 1982

His design ideas spring from an intensely personal vision, rather than seeking form through investigation of specific functional problems and resolving them by pushing the envelope of Modern materials technology. Graves' repertoire of materials is emphatically *de luxe,* often employing choice timbers or precious metals; even if mass produced, his designs refer to crafts traditions rather than mechanized production. One could say that his work is actually *anti-Modernist* in this respect, since it is not primarily concerned with designing good quality generic items for everyman (the implicit goal of Modern design), but with reclaiming the notion of the hand-made object, the elegant appurtenance.

While other architects of his generation have also turned their hand to design – one thinks particularly of Richard Meier, Charles Gwathmey, Robert Venturi and Frank Gehry, all of whom have designed for Swid Powell, for example – few have developed as comprehensive a range of artifacts and furnishings. For Graves, architecture and interiors are a continuum. "I never thought of buildings as being distinct from their interiors," he says. "That's part of the Rome influence. A room is set up around furniture the way buildings are set up around landscape." He cites a mentor, the veteran architectural theorist Colin Rowe, who asserts that it is easier to rearrange the furni-

From left to right
Corporate identity and packaging material for Lenox, 1988

Interior of the Lenox store in Palm Beach Gardens, Florida, 1988

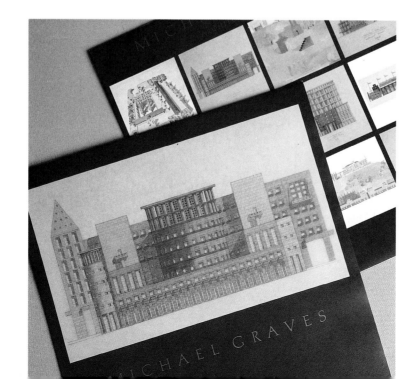

MICHAEL GRAVES
THE HUMANA BUILDING, LOUISVILLE, 1982

ture in a Classical house than a Modernist home, because the latter tends to require more *set-pieces* to sustain a sense of intimacy.

Following the success of the "Portland Building", and the "Humana Building" in Louisville, Kentucky, Graves' architectural work made a quantum leap. Suddenly his practice was commissioned to design skyscrapers, hotels and multi-use developments on urban tracts, and projects poured in from Japan.

As the scale of his architectural projects has grown, his enthusiasm for designing small-scale artifacts seems only to have increased. Old hands at the office joke about having to stand around, waiting patiently for approval on modifications to some multi-million dollar skyscraper, while Graves is immersed in detailing a new vase or clock.

Looking at the vast array of Graves' projects over the last decade, one can identify elements of a formal vocabulary which tend to crop up irrespective of the scale of the artifact. For example, the "Lucca" and "Urbino" wall sconces, manufactured by Baldinger, bear a strong family resemblance, in their cylindrical form girded by metal, to

Left
Te Neues *Landscape*. Art notecards, 1991-2

Te Neues *Architecture*. Art notecards, 1991-2

Te Neues calendar, 1991-2

Right
Poster of the Humana Building for Edition Lidiarte Publishers, 1993

131

the Alessi press-filter coffee pot, a glass vessel held in a metal portcullis. This basic drum form appears again, at much vaster scale, in several building projects, be it the original design for the Whitney Museum (where a perforated cylinder was to have served as a columnar seam between the Marcel Breuer building and Graves's addition, never realized) or the rotunda terminating the west end of the proposed 2121 Pennsylvania Avenue development.

Indeed, his product designs often have the look of miniaturized architecture: the birdhouse of 1987, explicitly, and the Alessi mantel clock of 1986 in birds eye maple with ebonised wood columns. There's a distinctly architectural presence even to the infamous Alessi kettle, the *conehead* for which Graves will remain known, long after the controversies over the "Portland Building", the "Whitney Extension" and the "Disney Headquarters" – with its giant "Seven Dwarfs" – have been forgotten.

Michael Graves is one of those rare originals in the art world. He created the classical "Michael" commemorative for the New Jersey Literary Hall of Fame, given to distinguished authors, and he designed the exciting and evolutionary Environmental Education Center at Liberty State Park overlooking the Statue of Liberty and the legendary Ellis Island Immigration Complex. There's no artistic challenge too small or too great for the multi-media maestro from Princeton.

Gordon
Bishop

Chairman of the New Jersey Literary Hall of Fame and editor at the "Newark Star Ledger", Newark, New Jersey

Some of the most attractive designs are those to be worn or held, attuned to the proportions of the human hand, the pleasure of touch, the sensuousness of materials used close to the skin. When asked how he tackles the shift in scale from designing buildings to designing portable artifacts, Graves replies that "it's more a question of tactility than a scale issue. When I was first thinking about the leather objects, I thought that the ones on the market felt awful, made of stuff one didn't care about". The series of desk books and personal documents in supple suede (by Spinneybeck) beg to be stroked, their gold embossed squares a finger-luring Braille. The watch for Cleto Munari and the flatware are dainty and almost feminine in their detailing; neither of them bear much kinship with trends in contemporary watch or cutlery design, and therein lies their charm, a willful antiquity.

High-rise commercial architecture in the 1980s essentially boiled down to designing the hat, boots, and overcoat, in other words, the penthouse suites, lobby (plus elevator cabs) and glazing/curtain walling. The floorplates of new skyscrapers were

Rome Reborn; the Vatican Library and Renaissance Culture. Design of the exhibition for the Library of Congress, Washington D.C., 1993

Costume designs for the production of *Fire*, Laura Dean for the Joffrey Ballet, New York, New York, 1982

machines for maximizing rentable square feet, undifferentiated shelves (around a service core) on which to stack contract furniture and tenants, in arrangements devised by their own interior design consultants.

Declining to submit to this traditional division of labor, Graves has reclaimed these orphan spaces as legitimately within the architect's sphere of attention. His diversification into architectural lighting and furnishings is a spin-off of his large commercial projects: the light fittings designed for the "Humana Building" appear, for example, in the Disney projects, customized with appropriate motifs, and elsewhere. Indeed, in the Disney hotels in Orlando, every surface comes under scrutiny, from the giant swans and dolphins on the roof to the oversized flower murals in the entrance lobby, the wallpaper along guestroom corridors, to the bedside lamps and cabinets. "It's an enormous accomplishment to get your furniture, rugs and lighting into a hotel room," says Graves, explaining the economics of the lodging business, which make it hard to compete with manufacturers who can produce knock-offs of original designs. "If someone, say in South Carolina or Toronto, can find the way to make a cut-price version, you can't beat them." But with his hotel track record – he's since completed the Hyatt Regency in Fukuoka, Japan and is nearing completion on the Astridplein in Antwerp – the Graves name has become a strategic marketing tool, a brand in its own right. "They want to use our furniture, to sell a Michael Graves room, not a Michael Graves-selected room."

With the end of the "Design Decade" – the Reagan/Bush era of conspicuous consumption – a more contemplative mood has hit America. Architecture, as handmaiden to the real estate industry, has suffered severely in the global recession. With the downturn in construction, there has been a discernible shift in design consciousness towards neglected issues of infrastructure, the environment, and provision for the disadvantaged. In the thickets of theory the debate has moved on even beyond "Deconstructivism", while that buzzword "Post-Modernism" is little heard and, as a movement, appears to have passed into history. For Graves, whose work was so closely identified with the aesthetic upheavals of the 1980s – indeed, whose buildings became the very beacons of debate in architecture – the cultural pendulum-swing poses dilemmas in terms of critical assessment.

Above
Cartoon for stage set for the production of *Fire*, Laura Dean for the Joffrey Ballet, New York, New York, 1982

Below
Detail of costume from the production of Fire, 1982

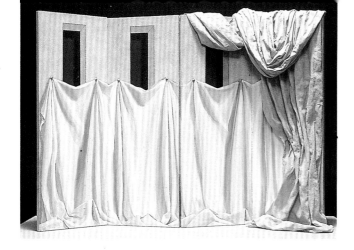

For a significant period in the early to mid-1980s, the Princeton School of Architecture was definitively Gravesian. (Many of his students spend time in his office after graduation, hence its affectionate nickname, "the finishing school".) With the arrival of younger faculty in the past few years the school's ideological direction has changed, towards critical theory and gender issues. Graves's once-dominant position on the faculty has therefore waned; one senses that this shift is disconcerting for him (cf. his remarks in the interview in this volume), the erstwhile *young Turk* now finding himself a member of the *old Guard*. But success as a built architect and accomplished product designer is perhaps inevitably at odds with a reputation as a radical.

Product design, like architecture, consists of variations on a theme. Michael's genius exists first in his choice of inspiration and second in his acute analysis of its elements and means of construction. I think that Michael's products reveal the most refined interpretions of his sources. Whether working from Etruscan vessel or ancient Roman jewelry, he both begins and ends with objects of beauty, unerring proportion and extraordinary craftmanship. The pleasure he takes in seeking each piece and then transforming it is contagious. One immediately begins to see artifacts with an enhanced appreciation, and for that I am certainly grateful.

Interior designer,
New York, New York

Above
Folding Screen for the Rizzoli Bookstore and Gallery, New York City, New York, 1984

Below
Scottish landscape, painting, 1986

To some, his focus on the formal and the visual – informed by his very particular synthesis of historical precedents – represents a reluctance to engage with issues currently high on the social agenda, and a retreat into a world of his own invention. To others, the consistency of Graves's aesthetic investigations and his prolific output are what mark him, indisputably, as an artist. Even if the media searchlight has, for now, moved on, that imaginary world is no less fecund, the Graves "Warehouse" a place of continuing development, those "Archaic Landscapes" as fertile as ever.

Tuscan landscapes, drawings, 1992-3

Biography

1934
Michael Graves was born on July 9, 1934 in Indiana-polis, Indiana, the son of a livestock broker and a nurse. He spent his childhood and youth in that town. At his mother's insistence, Michael Graves, who drew cartoons even as a young child, decided against becoming a painter. "Unless you can draw as well as Picasso, you had better become an engineer or architect."

1954
Michael Graves enrolls at the Department of Architecture of the University of Cincinnati, Ohio.

1955
While still a student he marries Gail Devine, a fashion designer and together they have two children, Sarah and Adam. At a later date, Michael and Gail divorce.

1958
Michael Graves receives his Bachelor of Architecture from Cincinnati and promptly registers as a graduate student at Harvard, where, in 1959, he is awarded a Master's Degree in Architecture.

1960
The young architect wins the "Prix de Rome" and consequently embarks on two years of study at the American Academy in Rome – he is currently a trustee of the academy. He subsequently settles in Princeton, initially working in the Modern tradition.

1962
Michael Graves starts teaching at Princeton University, New Jersey, first as a lecturer, finally as a full professor.

1964
He opens his own architecture studio in Princeton. Initially private commissions. Michael Graves is meanwhile known in academic circles: his paintings and articles reach a wider audience and he joins Peter Eisenman, Richard Meier, John Hejduk and Charles Gwathmey in the "Whites", who were also known as the "New York Five".

1967
He is awarded the first of over 45 New Jersey Society of Architects Design Awards for his "Oyster Bay Town Plan".

1969
Joint exhibition in the New York Museum of Modern Art.

1970
Michael Graves wins the Progressive Architecture Award for his "Rockefeller House". To date, he has received the prize a further 14 times.

1971
From 1971-7 he is Visiting Professor at the following: the University of Texas in Austin, the University of Houston, Texas, the New School for Social Research, New York and the University of California, Los Angeles.

1972
His design for the "Synderman House" in Fort Wayne, Indiana is representative of the new playful and decorative formal language and color scheme he developed in the early Seventies.
He marries Lucy James, who remains his wife until 1977.

1975
Michael Graves' search for a figurative self-explanatory architecture makes him a founder of Post-Modernism. The first example of this approach is the "Plocek Residence" in Warren Township, New Jersey.
He receives the first of a total of nine American Institute of Architects National Honor Awards for his design for the "Hanselmann House" in Fort Wayne, Indiana.

1977
He modernizes his own residence, the "Warehouse", in New Jersey. As its name suggests, the building is a former warehouse and has served Michael Graves for over 20 years as his own architectural laboratory. As of 1977 a simplification and consolidation of the elements he uses is to be imployed. He is increasingly mentioned in the national press and his designs now appear regularly on the title pages of the architectural press. He now starts designing products.

1979
His furniture and showrooms for Sunar are a commercial success. Michael Graves designs showrooms for the company in Chicago, Dallas, Houston, Los Angeles and New York, among other places.

1982
In the early Eighties he focuses increasingly on designing interiors, furniture, carpets, jewelry, lights and fabrics.

1983
Design of the "Humana Building" in Louisville, Kentucky.
With his plan for the "Portland Building" in Portland, Oregon, Michael Graves' name is forever established as synonymous with Post-Modernism. He also designs buildings all over the world, although above all in the United States and Japan.

1985
Design of a legendary kettle for Alessi. To be followed at a later date by further designs for the table.

1986-90
Michael Graves designs the "Dolphin" and "Swan" Hotels for Walt Disney World in Orlando, Florida.

1991
"Graves Design" is launched as the product design department of what has in the mean time become a well-established architectural office. The American Academy of Arts and Letters makes the architect and designer one if its members.

1994
Michael Graves opens his first store, in which he offers objects he has himself designed.
The architect and designer now has numerous private and public commissions for architectural work and interior design, for furniture and accessories designs throughout the world.
Michael Graves lives in Princeton, New Jersey.

Select Bibliography

There is no shortage of literature on Michael Graves. The lion's share of publications to date have been on his work as an architect, which is not the object of the present monograph. This book is the first monograph devoted specifically to Michael Graves' work as a designer. The bibliography was selected bearing this in mind. The aim was to compile a comprehensive list of articles on his products and interior design in the overall context of his work as a designer.

Books on Michael Graves

Peter Arnell, Ted Bickford, Karen Vogel Wheeler, (eds.): *Michael Graves, Buildings and Projects 1966-1981,* (Rizzoli, New York, 1987).
Charles Jencks: *Kings of Infinite Space: Michael Graves and Frank Lloyd Wright,* (Academy Editions, London, 1984).
Frampton, Kenneth: *Five Architects: Eisenman, Graves, Gwathmey, Hejduk, Meier,* (Oxford University Press, New York, 1975).
Karen Vogel Nichols; Patrick Burke, Caroline Hancock (eds.): *Michael Graves, Buildings and Projects 1982-1989,* (Princeton Architectural Press, New York, 1990).

Interviews with and Articles by Michael Graves

Michael Graves: *Architettura di mobili e tapetti,* in: *Modo* (I) December, 1980, pp. 41-5.
Michael Graves on Michael Graves: GA Interview, in: *GA Document 5* (J) (1982), pp. 4-12.

Portraits of Michael Graves

anon: Profile: Michael Graves, in: *Metropolitan Home* (USA), April, 1985.
anon, Hot Properties: Graves Braves the Nineties, in: *Metropolitan Home,* September/October, 1993.
Marlyn Bethany: The architect as artist, in: *New York Times Magazine,* April 25, 1982, p. 82.
John Morris Dixon, Sylvia Lavin: Michael Graves, Architect: Growth and Diversity, in: *Progressive Architecture* (USA), March, 1990.
Charles Gandee: The Prince of Princeton, in: *House & Garden* (USA), July, 1988, pp.132-9.
Paul Goldberger: Architecture of a different color, in: *New York Times Magazine* (USA), October 10, 1982.
Vera Graaf: Zeitgeist und Biedermeier, in: *Architektur & Wohnen,* March, 1991, pp. 23-30.
Robert Maxwell: The Individual Feeling for Collective Beauty, in: *Michael Graves, Buildings and Projects 1982-1989,* eds. Karen Vogel Nichols, Patrick Burke, Caroline Hancock (Princeton Architectural Press, New York, New York, 1990).
Pilar Viladas: The Taste of a Tastemaker, in: *Progressive Architecture* (USA), September, 1988, pp. 100-9.

Michael Graves in Postmodern Literature

Carpeting – Volker Fischer: *Bodenreform,* (Ernst & Sohn, Berlin, 1989), pp. 86-93
Michael Collins: *Post-Modern Design,* (Rizzoli, New York, 1990), pp. 123-77

Charles Jencks: The New International Style, in: *Domus* (I), March, 1983
Heinrich Klotz (ed.): *Die Revision der Moderne, Postmoderne Architektur 1960-1980,* (Exhibition catalogue German Architecture Museum, Prestel, Munich, 1984)
Andreas C. Papadakis, Michael Collins, Peter Fuller, Volker Fischer, Charles Jencks, Hans Hollein: *The Postmodern Object,* (Academy Group, London, 1988)

Individual Projects und Products

Alessi – Patrizia Scarzella: *Steel & Style, The Story of Alessi Householdware,* (Arcadia Edizioni, Milan (I), 1987)
Alessi – Laura Polinoro, Alberto Alessi, Alessandro Mendini: *Dieci anni di progetto 1980-1990,* (Alessi, Crusinallo (I), 1989)
Alessi clocks, Officina Alessi watches, (Alessi, Crusinallo (I), 1993), pp. 8-14
Award-winning products - Best of Category and Honorable Mention, in: *ID Annual Design Review* (USA), July/August, 1989, pp. 45 and 113
Furniture – Peter Dormer: *Die neuen Möbel,* (Kohlhammer, Stuttgart, 1987)
Furniture – Margaret Blythe Rennolds: *Furniture by Architects,* (Harry N. Abrams, New York, 1988), pp. 110-2
Diane von Furstenberg: Couture in a New Shop, in: *New York Times,* December, 1984
Graves Design Studio Store – anon: Would Retailing Suit Michaelangelo? in: New York Times, February, 1994
Interiors – Sylvia Lavin: Interiors Platform, in: *Interiors* (USA), February, 1988
Jewelry – Barbara Radice: *Jewelry by Architects,* (Rizzoli, New York, 1987), pp. 29-31
Memphis – Barbara Radice: *Memphis,* (Thames & Hudson, London, 1985)
Newark Museum – Peter C. Papademetriou: Four Not-so-easy Pieces, Newark Museum, New Jersey, in: *Progressive Architecture* (USA), March, 1990
Plocek residence – Charles Jencks: The Plocek Residence, in: *Architectural Digest* (USA), May, 1987
Porcelain – Annette Tapert: *Swid Powell, Objects by Architects,* (Rizzoli, New York, 1990), pp. 38-47
Sunar Furniture Showrooms. In: *GA Document 5,* (J) 1982, p. 16-35
Walt Disney – All that Fun…Mickey, Grande Urbaniste, in: *Architecture* (USA), June-July, 1992
Walt Disney – Marc Alden Branch: Story Time, in: *Progressive Architecture* (USA), March, 1990
Walt Disney – William Weathersby: Swan Lake, in: *Restaurant/Hotel Design* (USA), June, 1990

Index

The following list is designed to facilitate the use of this monograph as a reference work, enabling the reader to find quickly the persons, products and projects mentioned or shown in the book. This index also serves as a key to the statement to be found at intervals throughout the book.

Numbers in italic refers to illustrations.

Staff List/Index of Firms

Organizations of Michael Graves 1984-94

A successful designer and architect could never cope with all the contracts and projects he is involved in without being able to rely on the assistance either of a team of staff members or the services of free-lancers. The following therefore provides a list of those who have supported or continue to support his work at the "Graves Design" design studio but excludes staff members of his architectural studio.

Senior Designers
Alex Lee
Barry Richards
Donald Strum

Organization and Management
Susan Howard
Ann Johnston
Linda Kinsey
Sybil McKenna
Karen Nichols
Carole Nicholson

Design Assistants
Meryl Blinder
Susan Butcher
Roger Crowley
Becky Godshall
Stephanie Magdziak
Kiev Matwijcow
Andy McNabb
Don Menke
Mark Naden
Mary Ann Ray
Deborah Regh
Ani Rosskam
Lindsay Suter
Keat Tan
Kirsten Thoft
Leslie Wellman

Model Builders
Dean Acquaviva
Albert Chini
Rob Leach
Adam Zangrilli

It is not, nor could it be the intention of this book to provide a comprehensive presentation of all the products Michael Graves has designed. Further information on the objects described above can often be obtained in the form of data supplied by the manufacturer in the form of brochures and leaflets.
Given that many of the products presented here are still available, the following list is meant to assist readers in applying directly to the manufacturers for additional information.

Alessi
Via Privata Alessi, 6
28023 Crusinallo die Omegna (No)
Italy

Architectural Products
now manufactured by Gilbert International
459 South Calhoun Street
Fort Worth, Texas 76104
USA

Arkitektura
379 West Broadway, 4th Floor
New York, New York 10012
USA

Baldinger Architectural Lighting
19-02 Steinway Street
Astoria, New York 11105
USA

Belvedere Studio
5411 Meaders Lane
Dallas, Texas 75229
USA

Cleto Munari
Via Generale Chinotto 3
36100 Vicenza
Italy

Dorsey Collection
Graves Design
341 Nassau Street
Princeton, New Jersey 08540
USA

Fantasma
47-00 33rd Street
Long Island City, New York 11101
USA

Pierre Junod
Gurzelen 5
2502 Bienne
Switzerland

Markuse Corporation
10 Wheeling Avenue
Woburn, Massachusetts 01801
USA

Möller Design
P.O. Box 27789
Santa Ana, California 92799
USA

Sawaya & Moroni
Via Andegari 18
20121 Milan
Italy

Spinneybeck Design
105 Wooster Street
New York, New York 10012
USA

Steuben Glass
Fifth Avenue 56th Street
New York, New York 10022
USA

Swid Powell
213 East 49th Street
New York, New York 10017
USA

The Walt Disney Company
500 South Buena Vista Street
Burbank, California 91521
USA

te Neues Verlag
Am Selder 37
47906 Kempen
Germany

Vecta Al
150 East, 58th Street
New York, New York 10155
USA

Vorwerk & Co. Teppichwerke
Kuhlmannstraße 11
31785 Hameln
Germany

Waechtersbacher Keramik
Fabrikstraße 12
63636 Brachttal
Germany

About the Authors

Aldo Rossi

is one of the most important Post-Modern architects. He initially made a name for himself as a teacher, theorist and later also editor of the *Casabella* journal (1955-64). He started his academic career in 1969 at Milan's Politecnico, followed by positions in Venice and Zurich. His main interest was in town planning and the relation between architecture and urban space. His fame as a practical architect was certain with projects such as San Cataldo cemetery in Modena, Italy and the Il Palazzo Hotel in Fukuoka, Japan. In 1991 he received the Pritzker Prize, probably the most important architectural prize awarded. In the area of product design his furniture lines for Molteni and his "La cupola" espresso pot for Alessi are no doubt best known. He lives and works in Milan.

Michael Collins

studied history and art history at the University of London. From 1979 to 1986 he was curator of the Modern Collection at the British Museum in London and above all became known for his numerous publications on Post-Modernism. His two books *Towards Post-Modernism* and *Post-Modern Design* were especially well-received. Michael Collins currently teaches at the University of Notre Dame and Kingston University, London.

Rainer Krause

used his company Anthologie Quartett to introduce numerous important representatives of international design to Germany in the 1980s. By profession a pharmacist and collector of design, since 1983 he has been German correspondent for *Casa Vogue,* the Italian journal. In 1988 he founded design…connections, a consultancy for corporate identity and corporate design. In 1990 he was in charge of selecting the collection for the "mus'ign" design museum at Castle Hollwinkel in Lower Saxony. He has created numerous exhibitions, edited catalogues, and written countless articles on design and architecture. He lives in Bad Essen, Germany.

Laura Cerwinske

is the well-known author of various successful publications on architecture, interior design, art and the applied arts. She first made a name for herself with *Tropical Deco: The Architecture and Design of Old Miami Beach* and later, the first comprehensive illustrated book on the subject *Russian Imperial Style*. Moreover, she has contributed regularly to various renowned architectural journals, such as *Progressive Architecture* and *Architectural Digest*. Laura Cerwinske lives and works in Miami, Florida and New York City.

Janet Abrams

works as a freelance critic and curator specialising in architecture, design and multimedia. She has written for numerous publications in the United States and Europe, including *The Independent*, *Archis*, and *Sight and Sound*. In 1989 she was awarded a doctorate in architectural history by Princeton University, where she had served as US correspondent for the British journal *Blueprint*, of which she was later appointed guest editor. Between 1991 and 1992 she was director of the Chicago Institute for Architecture and Urbanism. Janet Abrams lives in New York, and is currently writer-at-large for *ID*, the International Design magazine.

Janet Abrams

Laura Cerwinske

Aldo Rossi

Rainer Krause

Michael Collins

Photo Credits

All due effort has been made to find out who held the copyright to the various photos displayed in this book. We would like to apologize in advance should we have left someone out and would be happy to include the correct entries in later editions. Please send information to: design...connections, Hanauer Landstraße 161-173, 60314 Frankfurt on Main, Germany.
The sequence of the names corresponds with the sequence of picture captions on the respective pages.

front cover: W. Taylor
back cover: S. Barker
p. 13: Paschall/Taylor
p. 18: Paschall/Taylor
p. 19: Proto Acme Photo, Paschall/Taylor, Richard Speedy
p. 20: E. Zeschin
p. 21: O. Gili, Paschall/'Taylor
p. 22: Acerbis, Alessi
p. 23: W. Taylor, W. Taylor
p. 24: W. Taylor, Paschall/Taylor
p. 25: W. Taylor, W. Taylor
p. 26: W. Taylor, W. Taylor
p. 27: Vorwerk
p. 28: Vorwerk
p. 29: Paola Mattioli (portrait)
p. 30: J. Goldberg/Esto
p. 31: T. Hursley
p. 32: W. Taylor, W. Taylor
p. 33: Proto Acme, W. Taylor
p. 35: W. Taylor
p. 36: Baldinger
p. 37: Baldinger, Baldinger
p. 38: W. Taylor, W. Taylor
p. 39: M. Bulaj
p. 40: S. Brooke
p. 41: J. Goldberg/Esto, J. Goldberg/Esto
p. 42: S. Brooke,
p. 43: M. Bulaj
p.44: T. Galliher
p. 45: Leigh Photographic Group, Arkitektura
p. 47: Leigh Photographic Group, Arkitektura
p. 48: W. Taylor
p. 49: W. Taylor
p. 50: S. Brooke
p. 51: S. Brooke, W. Taylor
p. 52: S. Brooke, Walt Disney (portrait)
p. 53: S. Brooke
p. 54: W. Taylor, W. Taylor, W. Taylor
p. 55: W. Taylor
p. 56: W. Taylor, W. Taylor
p. 57: S. Brooke, S. Brooke, S. Brooke
p. 58: W. Taylor
p. 59: W. Taylor, W. Taylor, S. Brooke
p. 60: W. Taylor, W. Taylor
p. 61: W. Taylor, W. Taylor
p. 62: W. Taylor, W. Taylor
p. 63: W. Taylor, W. Taylor, W. Taylor (portrait)
p. 82: W. Taylor
p. 83: W. Taylor
p. 84: Alessi
p. 85: W. Taylor
p.86: W. Taylor

p. 87: W. Taylor
p. 88: W. Taylor, W. Taylor
p. 89: Alessi, Alessi, W. Taylor
p. 90: Alessi
p. 91: W. Taylor
p. 92: W. Taylor
p. 93: M. Bulaj, M. Bulaj, M. Bulaj
p. 94: Alessi, Alessi
p. 95: Alessi, Alessi
p. 96: M. Hales
p. 97: W. Taylor, W. Taylor
p. 98: D. Sweeney, W. Taylor
p. 99: W. Taylor, W. Taylor
p. 101: W. Taylor, W. Taylor
p. 102: Steuben Glass, Paschall/Taylor
p. 103: Paschall/Taylor, Steuben Glass
p. 104: W. Taylor, WMF
p. 105: Munari
p. 107: M. Bulaj, M. Bulaj
p. 108: W. Taylor, W. Taylor
p. 109: W. Taylor
p. 110: W. Taylor, W. Taylor, Carillon Importers Ltd./TBWA
p. 111: M. Bulaj, M. Bulaj
p. 112: W. Taylor, W. Taylor
p. 113: T&E, T&E, W. Taylor
p. 114: M. Bulaj
p. 117: O. Gili
p. 118: W. Taylor, O. Gili
p. 119: O. Gili
p. 120: H. Evans, M. Bulaj
p. 121: W. Taylor, Paschall/Taylor, H. Evans
p. 122: Paschall/Taylor, Paschall/Taylor
p. 123: M. Bulaj, W. Taylor
p. 124: W. Taylor
p. 125: B. Blushon, B. Blushon
p. 126: W. Taylor, W. Taylor
p. 128: W. Taylor, W. Taylor
p. 129: K. Sargent
p. 130: M. Bulaj, M. Bulaj, M. Bulaj
p. 132: S. Brooke
p. 133: S. Brooke, S. Brooke
p. 135: H. Migdoll
p. 136: D. Cronen, R. H. Hensleigh
p. 137: M. Bulaj, M. Bulaj
p. 142: F. Brunetti (A. Rossi), D. Phelps (L. Cerwinske), J. Edelstein (J. Abrams)

© 1994 Ernst & Sohn
Verlag für Architektur und technische
Wissenschaften GmbH, Berlin
ISBN 3-433-02550-9
Ernst & Sohn is a member of the
VCH Publishing Group.
All rights reserved, especially those of
translation into other languages.
Printed in Germany

Distributed in North America to the trade,
for Academy Group Limited,
by St. Martins Press, 175 Fifth Avenue,
New York, N.Y. 10010
ISBN 1-85490-903-7

Design: Heine/Lenz/Zizka
Outside Editor: Petra Schmidt
Translation: Jeremy Gaines